Celtic Mythology
A Captivating Guide to the Gods, Sagas and Beliefs

Written by the Creator of the Captivating History Series:

Matt Clayton

© Copyright 2017

All rights Reserved. No part of this book may be reproduced in any form without permission in writing from the author. Reviewers may quote brief passages in reviews.

Disclaimer: No part of this publication may be reproduced or transmitted in any form or by any means, mechanical or electronic, including photocopying or recording, or by any information storage and retrieval system, or transmitted by email without permission in writing from the publisher.

While all attempts have been made to verify the information provided in this publication, neither the author nor the publisher assumes any responsibility for errors, omissions or contrary interpretations of the subject matter herein.

This book is for entertainment purposes only. The views expressed are those of the author alone, and should not be taken as expert instruction or commands. The reader is responsible for his or her own actions.

Adherence to all applicable laws and regulations, including international, federal, state and local laws governing professional licensing, business practices, advertising and all other aspects of doing business in the US,

Canada, UK or any other jurisdiction is the sole responsibility of the purchaser or reader.

Neither the author nor the publisher assumes any responsibility or liability whatsoever on the behalf of the purchaser or reader of these materials. Any perceived slight of any individual or organization is purely unintentional.

Contents

FREE BONUS FROM CAPTIVATING HISTORY (AVAILABLE FOR A LIMITED TIME) 6

INTRODUCTION 7

CHAPTER 1 — CELTIC ANIMISM 13

CHAPTER 2 — UNIVERSAL CELTIC GODS 20

CHAPTER 3 — LOCAL IRISH CELT GODS 36

CHAPTER 4 — LOCAL GALLIC CELT GODS 61

CHAPTER 5 — CELTIC SAGAS: THE CYCLES 69

CHAPTER 6 — CELTIC BELIEFS: ANIMAL AND HUMAN SACRIFICE 85

CHAPTER 7 — CELTIC BELIEFS: REINCARNATION 95

CHAPTER 8 — CELTIC BELIEFS: MATRIARCHY 100

CONCLUSION – WHAT WE HAVE LEARNED ... 109

PREVIEW OF NORSE MYTHOLOGY 113
A FASCINATING GUIDE TO UNDERSTANDING THE SAGAS, GODS, HEROES, AND BELIEFS OF THE VIKINGS 113

INTRODUCTION—CLIMATE CHANGE MADE THEM RUTHLESS 113

PART 1—HEROES AND SAGAS 117

CHAPTER 1—THE ICELANDIC SAGAS 118

Preview of Egyptian Mythology 127
Captivating Stories of the Gods, Goddesses, Monsters and Mortals 127

INTRODUCTION: EGYPT IN CONTEXT 127

Preview of Greek Mythology 137
A Captivating Guide to the Ancient Gods, Goddesses, Heroes and Monsters 137

INTRODUCTION 137

CHAPTER 1 — URANUS: BETRAYAL BY CRONUS 142

FREE BONUS FROM CAPTIVATING HISTORY (AVAILABLE FOR A LIMITED TIME) 149

Free Bonus from Captivating History (Available for a Limited time)

Hi History Lovers!

Now you have a chance to join our exclusive history list so you can get your first history ebook for free as well as discounts and a potential to get more history books for free! Simply visit the link below to join.

Captivatinghistory.com/ebook

Also, make sure to follow us on:

Twitter: @Captivhistory

Facebook: Captivating History: @captivatinghistory

Introduction

The Celts were a people who lived throughout central Europe from about the 500s BC to the AD 700s. The exact origins of their culture and of their extent at any one time is unknown. There is some evidence they existed in Eastern Europe, the Balkans, and even in central Anatolia (modern-day Turkey). We also have evidence they inhabited Ireland and western Iberia.

Besides being called Celts by modern scholars, the peoples were called many other names. Those living in what is modern France, and who spilled over into western Germany and northern Italy, were called Gauls and their language and beliefs called "Gallic." The Irish Celts were called Gaels, and their culture called "Gaelic." The people were also called Milesians.

Very little is known directly from the Celts themselves. Almost everything we know about them comes from their enemies, and those people had little motivation to portray the Celts in a favorable light. Did the Celts believe in human sacrifice? Quite simply, we don't know. Julius Caesar said they did. Cicero, Suetonius, and Lucan also suggested this was true. But too often an enemy will say bad things about their foe to justify anything they may wish to do to them. They will demonize a people so their troops will be galvanized to win against them no matter what it takes.

The Roman emperors Tiberius and Claudius outlawed the practice of human sacrifice, so there may be some validity to the claims. Yet, those emperors could merely have been reacting to rumors instead of hard evidence. We simply do not know for certain.

We know the Celts had many strange practices — strange to us, that is. For instance, they would proudly display the heads of their enemies after chopping them off. They had religious leaders, called Druids, who supposedly had magical powers.

We also know when the Celts of Gaul were conquered, they retained some of their culture, but it became heavily mixed with the social customs and beliefs of the Romans. So, deciphering what were pure Celtic beliefs remains a difficult task.

The Celts had numerous gods which the writers of other cultures frequently associated with their own pantheons. But we also know the Celts revered nature and may very well have started as animists. According to the Cambridge dictionary, animism means, "the belief that all natural things, such as plants, animals, rocks, and thunder, have spirits and can influence human events."

We will explore the various aspects of Celtic gods, sagas and beliefs, gaining a general overall picture of their culture. We'll attempt to bring some of their stories to life so all the details are more than merely a bunch of dry facts. We will enter their world and recreate it in as much detail as possible, from the little bit we know for certain, combined with ancillary facts from the various sciences.

Meteorologically, for example, we know, for instance, the Celtic culture first made itself known to us about the middle of a relatively cool period between the Minoan Warm Period, circa 1000 BC, and the Roman Warm Period, circa AD 1. That cool period was somewhat warmer than our current Modern Warm Period, despite what you may have heard from the popular press and some political organizations. This means there was a relatively moderate level of prosperity for almost everyone, including the Celts. There were two very brief periods when the climate cooled down to the level of our modern warmth, according to the Greenland ice core temperature proxies. These may have stimulated migration, especially if the relative prosperity had allowed their core culture to expand beyond the home environment's ability to support their growing numbers.

At their greatest extent, about 275 BC, the climate was already well above the warmth of the Medieval Warm Period and well on its way to the heady prosperity of the Roman Warm Period. Still, it was nothing like the earlier Minoan Warm Period. From that relative high point, global climate has experienced a strong cooling trend ever since, down to today. So, it was within the "foothills of warmth" that the Celts expanded across all of Europe.

At the Celt's greatest extent, the Romans had not yet expanded beyond the Italian peninsula. Rome's Punic Wars were not to start for another decade or so. The Celts possessed what is today northern Italy and most of France. And it is in this region that we are able to gain many of our most significant insights into the world of the Celts.

What's Ahead in the Book

In the first chapter, we tackle the Celtic love of nature and their relationship with the trees, lakes, mountains and other elements of the natural world. We'll gain an understanding why Celtic culture has become so popular in our modern world. More people are returning to nature and a more natural way of doing things, so this makes a knowledge of all things Celtic even more attractive.

In the second chapter, we'll look at the universal gods of Celtic religion. Though these may have come after their period of animism (simple, yet spiritual reverence for the elements of nature), these gods and goddesses were common enough across all Celtic cultures to give us a cohesive ingredient that unifies our understanding of their society.

Next, in chapter three, we will look at local Irish gods and, perhaps, gain a greater appreciation for Ireland and its culture. We'll peer into the fascinating and frequently dangerous world of Gaelic rivalries. We will learn how several waves of invasions had beset the Emerald Isle with wars, death, and renewal. We will learn of the early gods of darkness and light and how they sometimes negotiated an uneasy peace.

In chapter four, we explore the nature of the Gallic gods that ruled over the enemies of Julius Caesar. We will even relive a semi-historical event which led one Roman tribune to gain a healthy respect for one of the Celtic goddesses — a female divinity whose name meant "battle crow."

In chapter five, we learn of the conniving female ruler Medb, who chose many husbands to serve on the throne of Connacht with her. And then we explore the Celtic sagas, starting with The Mythological Cycle of Celtic legend.

Then, we touch on The Ulster Cycle, followed by The Fenian Cycle, ending with The Cycles of the Kings, also known as the Historical Cycle.

In chapter six, we peer into the dark realm of animal and human sacrifice. Though we don't know much about this and its validity, we'll expand on what is known to see if we can make sense of the legends.

Chapter seven covers the Celtic belief in reincarnation — a belief that many who have not studied history seem to think belongs only in Eastern philosophy. But no, even Julius Caesar marveled at their strong belief in the immortal soul and its ability to return to this world in another human form.

Chapter eight enters the mysterious world of Celtic matriarchy — the controversial topic of female rule.

With each chapter, we take a fanciful glimpse into the very personal world of the Celts. Each narrative attempt to help us understand the Celtic viewpoint and why their beliefs held such powerful relevance in their society.

Thanks for your interest in Celtic mythology and their gods, sagas and beliefs. Now, let us start that exploration.

Chapter 1 — Celtic Animism

Bradán made his way down to the stream, carrying a spear in one hand and clutching the brush with the other to keep himself from slipping. Behind him, Mochán and Cadeyrn followed. At a level area next to the stream, Bradán stopped and squatted, bowing his head. With eyes closed, he reached into his pouch and withdrew a wand.

The younger men joined their middle-aged leader, also squatting and bowing their heads in reverence. The bright summer sun warmed their shoulders as they prayed.

"Sruth suthain," he said softly, extending the wand toward the stream. The words meant "stream eternal."

"Sruth suthain," the other two repeated.

"Blessed be thy sacred waters," continued Bradán, "for they sanctify the land. Please bless our efforts to take from your bounty so that we may find sustenance for life."

They did not have a Druid with them to make their actions holy, so they did the next best thing — performing the ritual as best they could to keep a balance with nature.

Bradán kept his head bowed in silence for nearly a minute longer. Several times, Mochán, the youngest of the three at 13 seasons, peeked up at their leader to see if he was done. To him, Bradán looked old, though he was only 35. The other man was a visitor from the continent and only 21.

Éiru was rich with forests and streams. Some of the ancient tales spoke of a time when the seas were far lower and the island had been part of the continent. During those times, a great ice wall had been rapidly receding from the land, making way for the coming of man.

The earliest inhabitants were kindred of the Euskara to the south, on the continental peninsula. They had heard these things, but only dimly understood what they meant. They had also heard of a time when their Druids could perform magic, communing with the trees—the oak, ash, apple, hazel, alder, elder and yew. They could also connect to the mountains, lakes, and streams in a way that had become forgotten.

At times, Bradán felt awkward performing the prayers before a hunt. He knew it was the right thing to do, but he almost always feared he might be doing it all wrong. Many times in the past, while watching the Druids perform these rites, he had sensed their own lack of faith as they mechanically performed by rote the prayers their society required of them.

Finally, he opened his eyes, saw Mochán glancing at him. The older man smiled back at the young one.

"Your nephew tells me we're not far," said Cadeyrn.

Bradán nodded. "Less than a day."

"And it's near a sacred hill?"

Again, Bradán nodded. "Cnoc na Teamhrach, what some call 'the Hill of Tara.' But now let us descend into silence, otherwise our prayer is for naught."

At that, Bradán rose and entered the stream slowly, moving one foot and then the next, inching toward the rocks where a fish might be sunning itself. He spotted one and raised his spear, gauging the water for its diffraction.

Suddenly, he lunged forward, driving the sharp, wooden stick into the fish, bringing it up, flailing on its pointed end.

Mochán shrieked with delight. Bradán had speared his favorite kind of fish.

Bradán threw him a glare that quickly subdued the youngster's enthusiasm. The leader moved the fish closer and, with his other hand, grasped the dying creature, forcing it more securely down the shaft. Then he held it aloft and said, "It is done. Sruth noíbaid íasco." The words meant, "the stream sanctifies the fish."

He nodded his head for another brief prayer and then turned back to the other two. "Let us in all humility prepare this fish to feed our bodies. May we thank both the stream and the fish for their contribution."

"Yes!" said Mochán with renewed excitement. "Firewood?"

Bradán smiled and nodded.

Cadeyrn chuckled at the boy's strong emotion. "Reminds me of my sister's boy, back in Gaul."

"Yes, and they also live at Avara Cathair?"

"The very same town. And are there any towns on Éiru?"

"None like yours. All of our settlements are crude by comparison —thatch, mud, and rough stones."

"But your hill is sacred."

"Yes," said Bradán and took a deep breath. "Our Druids say it is the most sacred hill on the entire island. Our greatest kings are sanctified there. The spirit of the hill is strong."

"I look forward to being there," replied Cadeyrn.

Moments later, the two men heard Mochán return with a loud "Whoop!"

He had returned with an arm full of dry twigs and branches, but had slipped and sat squarely on his back end with a startled look in his eyes.

Both men roared with laughter at the comical sight.

Characters and Name Meanings

Cadeyrn (male name meaning "battle king." Ancient Celtic)

Bradán (male name meaning "salmon." Ancient Irish)

Mochán (male name meaning "little early one." Ancient Irish)

Reverence for the Spirits

Celtic culture held the natural world in high regard. After all, nature was powerful, mysterious, and vitally important for their survival. Like so many other cultures of the ancient and primitive worlds, they attempted to understand the forces of nature and to control or perhaps appease them.

These people remained confident that they could gain a rapport with the spirits of nature.

This way, they could increase the chances of their own survival.

Through rituals and offerings, the humans could acquire the proper balance with nature so selfishness — the spirit of ego — would not pollute their future with disaster. Every supernatural force needed to be appeased. This required proper humility, which is the opposite of egoism. Each Celtic citizen knew that spirit was interwoven with the material world, much as the spirit of man is interwoven with his mortal body.

For the Celts, a separate spirit possessed every rocky outcrop, marsh, bog, spring, river, tree, and mountain.

Unlike the polytheistic religions of the Etruscans, Greeks and Romans, Celtic culture was rural and animistic. Those other cultures were urban with anthropomorphic gods and goddesses, as well as other physical, god-like monsters. To the Celts, the spirit was non-physical, but it had its own affinities for the physical aspects of the material world.

Certain locations were considered sacred and imbued with powerful spirits. Such locations were considered to be sanctuaries, safe from the more brutal realities of the physical realm.

From time to time, Celtic people would make offerings to the spirits of a place, depositing their foodstuffs, weapons, jewelry, or other valuables in specially designated pits or bodies of water. Each donation connected the person to the land in a way that made the person and the spirit responsible for each other.

Water spirits were considered powerful for their ability to connect this world with the realm of spirit — the "other world" of the dead, and those waiting to be reborn into this world. Water was a giver of life.

Natural springs from which rivers were born were revered by healers.

The Celts also deeply respected the wind, rain, and thunder.

From the animal kingdom, Celts deeply respected and admired animals for their traits and skills. Dogs were good in the hunt, snakes could shed their skin and thus be reborn, and beavers were experts building with wood.

Hunting spirits were viewed by the Celts not so much as helpers in a successful hunt, but arbiters who kept a balance between man and the animal kingdom. In some respects, this is exactly what the Greek goddesses Diana and Artemis did in their culture. A Celtic hunter would never go hunting without the permission of the appropriate spirit.

Chapter 2 — Universal Celtic Gods

Boudicca wiped her upper lip with the back of her hand. Exertion and the hot, summer day had her sweating profusely. She lightly touched the gold torc wrapped around her neck — a symbol of royal authority amongst her people. The rigid neck ring was intricately decorated with symbols representing the spirits. On the front of her torc, where the two ends met, one end was embossed with the tiny image of three women — the máthair or matronae. The other end had embossed a tiny image of Epona, the horse goddess, and goddess of fertility.

As a middle-aged woman of noble birth, she might not otherwise have been leading a hundred thousand of her own people, the Iceni, along with the Trinovantes and others.

But here she was, fighting to restore the birthright of her two daughters who had been cheated by the patriarchal Romans and their laws that said women could not inherit.

She had already killed thousands of them at Camulodunum, at a place that would one day be called Colchester. Now, she and her men were heading toward the relatively new settlement of Londinium — what would one day become known as London. Now, they had happened upon a patrol of Roman soldiers.

She looked back as she heard the others approach. The old man was Haerviu — a little too old to live up to his name of "battle worthy." It was doubtful that he would survive the coming fight.

Lugubelenus was a brash young man who had already made several advances against one of her daughters, and fancied himself to be a leader, apparently trying to live up to his own name.

Teutorigos was the last to arrive. His name meant "ruler of the people," and he had great potential for that, but lacked any interest in such things.

"By Epona," she whispered loudly. "You're all late. The Romans are starting to leave."

"Perhaps we should let them," replied Teutorigos quietly. "Do we really want to fight with them, here?"

"They keep offending the gods," said Haerviu. "building their roads and monstrous structures in the middle of sacred places. Besides, they are thieves who cheated the two princesses out of their inheritance."

"Yes, well, the gods should be able to take care of such assaults on their own."

Lugubelenus, glanced at Boudicca and lifted his chin a bit.

"This is not the time for discussion," replied Boudicca. "Yes, they keep doing those things, but this is about them not honoring their commitment to my late husband and to our tradition that allows women — my daughters, damn it! — to receive their inheritance."

"May Cernunnos guide us," said Haerviu. "We don't do these things for our own selfish needs, but for the greater good of the natural world, of which we are a part."

"Well said, Haerviu," replied Boudicca. "May the three mothers protect us in what we are about to do."

"But when do we attack?" asked Teutorigos.

Boudicca flashed him a wily grin. "Now!"

Characters and Name Meanings

Boudicca (female name meaning "victory" in ancient Celtic). She was a Celtic queen of Britain.

Haerviu (male name meaning "battle worthy." A Breton form of Harvey).

Lugubelenus (male name possibly meaning "leader." Ancient Celtic, possibly an older form of the Welsh name Llywelyn).

Teutorigos (a male name meaning, "ruler of the people." Ancient Celtic, older form of Tudor).

The Most Widely Known Celtic Gods and Goddess

Over time, and with increased associations with the Etruscans, Phoenicians, Ancient Greeks, and later Romans, the Celts grew to "materialize" their spirits into more anthropomorphic gods and goddesses.

Not all the gods and goddesses mentioned here were known throughout the Celtic world. Those mentioned in this chapter were at least considered "supra-regional" — worshipped across more than one region. This meant that they were more popular. And since a lack of evidence never proves they were unknown in other regions, we may one day discover evidence that some or all of these were even more widely known.

Across most of the Celtic world, the *Matres* and *Matronae* were worshipped throughout the period of the Roman Empire. Almost always, they were depicted on altars and votive offerings as a group of three goddesses — the "mother" goddesses. These divine beings were similar in some respects to the *dísir* and the Valkyries of Norse mythology, and the Fates of Greek mythology. *Dea*

Matrona means "divine mother goddess" and this name was sometimes used in place of *Matres* and *Matronae*. *Dea Matrona* was also the source name for the river Marne in Gaul.

Toutatis (also Teutates) was considered to have been a tribal protector for the Celts of Gaul and Britain. In Roman Britain, finger rings with the initials "TOT" were common, and were thought to refer to the god Toutatis. Some scholars think the Romans associated Toutatis with their own god, Mercury. In fact, Julius Caesar said Mercury was the Celts' most esteemed god and that images of him were to be found throughout the Celtic territory. To the Celtic "Mercury" were attributed the functions of "inventor of all the arts," protector of merchants and travelers, and the preeminent god for everything concerning commercial gain. Toutatis could have been one aspect of a triune god named Lugus.

Caesar also mentioned the Celts of Gaul paid homage to Apollo because he rid them of disease. They honored Mars, who ruled over all the things of war. They revered Jupiter, who oversaw the heavens. And they honored Minerva, who remained patroness of handicrafts. Julius Caesar also mentioned that the Celtic Gauls all claimed to be descended from Dīs Pater, which was a Roman god of the underworld. Likely what he meant was the Gauls claimed to be from a god who resembled Dīs Pater in some way — perhaps a subterranean god associated with prosperity and fertility.

Alaunus was a god of healing and prophecy, which were two traits of Apollo (both as a Greek and Roman god).

Alisanos may have been a mountain god, or may have been related to the alder tree.

Andarta was a warrior goddess with evidence of her worship in Bern, Switzerland and in southern France.

Anextiomarus (female form, Anextiomara) has been associated with the Roman god Apollo, with dedications found throughout France and Switzerland.

Artio was a bear goddess. Her worship was centered around Bern, Switzerland.

Aveta was a mother goddess worshipped across a region which included parts of France, Germany and Switzerland.

Belenus was a sun god, associated with horses, and thought to ride across the sky in a horse-drawn chariot, pulling the sun along with it. His consort was thought to be the Celtic goddess Belisama, frequently associated with Minerva.

Borvo was a god involved in healing, minerals and bubbling spring water. Whenever associated with a Roman god, Borvo was always paired with Apollo.

The Celtic goddess **Brigantia** was associated with Roman Victoria and remains a cognate with Irish Brigit.

Camulus was another Celtic god associated with Mars. In one stone carving, he is portrayed with a wreath of oak. In another location, he was shown with a ram head wearing horns. His name may have been the basis of Camelot — the legendary city of King Arthur fame.

Cathubodua was a Celtic goddess and possible cognate of the Irish Babd Catha. Her name meant "battle crow." Several goddesses share the same root, which means either "victory" or "fighting." Because of this, she would be comparable to goddesses in other cultures—Victoria (Roman), Nike (Greek) and Sigyn (Norse).

Cernunnos was a horned god of life, fertility, wealth, animals, and the realm of the underworld. He is shown with stag antlers, sometimes carrying a coin purse. Most of the time he is seen seated cross-legged. He is also shown wearing torcs or holding them in his hands.

Cicolluis was the "Great-Breasted" god of strength, associated with Mars. This god has sometimes been associated with Cichol Gricenchos of Irish Celtic myth.

Cissonius is yet another Celtic god associated with Mercury. In fact, he is second only to Visucius in such associations. In attempting to understand his name, linguists have interpreted it as meaning "carriage-driver" or "courageous." From this, they suspect that he was a patron of trade and the protector of those who traveled. Thus, the association with Mercury seems to be a good fit. There is also a minor note of a goddess named Cissonia, but the relationship to this god is unknown.

Condatis — a name which means "waters meet" — is a Celtic god related to rivers, especially where they come together. He is associated with Roman god Mars, likely through his divine healing powers.

Damona is a Celtic goddess. According to one scholar, her name means "divine cow" — from Celtic "damos" which means "cow." In two different regions, she is seen with a divine consort — Apollo Borvo in one, and Apollo Moritasgus in another.

Epona was a goddess of fertility, plus a protector of horses, ponies, donkeys, and mules. She was one of the most widely worshipped Celtic deities. Some scholars feel she may have been associated with the dead, leading them to the "otherworld" on a pony.

Evidence of her worship has been found in Britain, throughout Gaul, modern Germany, and the Roman provinces of the River Danube. One inscription in Germany was made by someone from the region of ancient Syria.

Erecura (also spelled Aerecura) a Celtic goddess associated with the Roman goddess of the underworld, Proserpina (also known in Greek as Persophone). Evidence of her worship has been found in modern Belgium, southeastern France, southwestern Germany, eastern Austria, northeastern Italy, and central Romania. Along with her symbols of the underworld, she is frequently seen with a cornucopia or an apple basket — symbols of fertility. Though the Celts revered this goddess across a broad territory, scholars doubt the name was Celtic in origin. One researcher suggested the name was Illyrian in origin.

Esus (also spelled Hesus and Aisus) is a Celtic god. He was depicted cutting branches from a willow tree with his blade. One intellectual suggests that his name derives from the Indo-European root for "well-being, passion and energy." The willow tree may represent the "Tree of Life." He could have been one part of a triune god, Lugus.

Grannus was a Celtic god of spas — healing mineral and thermal springs. He was also associated with the sun, and thus frequently associated with Apollo as Apollo Grannus. His worship was also frequently associated with the Celtic god Sirona and sometimes the Roman god Mars. Perhaps the most famous center for worshipping Grannus can be found near the modern city of Aachen, Germany, that country's westernmost municipality. In ancient times, the hot springs there was called Aquae Granni. Roman Emperor Caracalla (AD 188–217) was said to have visited there with votive offerings and prayers to be healed.

Ialonus Contrebis (or Ialonus and Gontrebis) was either a Celtic god or two gods. The first part — Ialonus — seems to come from a root meaning "clearing."

Lenus was the Celtic god of healing, frequently associated with the Roman god Mars. He was particularly important to the Treveri tribe in what is now western Germany. Unlike most syncretized names combining Celtic with Roman divinity, most inscriptions show "Lenus Mars" rather than "Mars Lenus." Quite often, he is pictured wearing a Greek Corinthian helmet.

Litavis (also Litauis) was a Celtic goddess sometimes associated with the Gallo-Roman syncretized god, Mars Cicolluis, suggesting that she may have been his consort. Some scholars consider her to be an earth goddess with a name derived from language roots meaning "to spread out flat."

Loucetios was a Celtic god whose name meant "lightning." He was invariably associated with Mars as Mars Loucetios, and frequently associated with the goddess Gallic Nemetona or the Roman goddess Victoria. He was known throughout the Rhine River Valley region, from Austria and Switzerland, through German, France, Liechtenstein and the Netherlands. Inscriptions to this god have also been found in Angers, western France, and in Bath, England.

Lugus is a Celtic god whose name remains a cognate with the Irish god Lugh. Though his name is rarely mentioned directly, his importance is implied by the proliferation of place names which seem to pay homage to him. His name seems to come from the Proto-Indo-European roots "to break" and "to swear an oath." A three-headed image found in Paris and Reims was thought to represent Lugus and also to be associated with the Roman god Mercury. Linguists suggest his name was the basis for the following location names:

- Lugdunum (modern Lyon, France)
- Loudun and Montluçon in France
- Loudoun, Scotland

- Dinlleu, Wales
- Leiden, Netherlands
- Lugones, Asturias, Spain
- Legnica, Silesia
- Lothian, Scotland
- Luton, England

One scholar suggests Lugus was a triune god, as represented by the three-headed image, representing Esus, Toutatis, and Taranis.

Maponos was a Celtic god with a name that meant "great son." He was equated with the Roman god Apollo.

Mogons was a Celtic god frequently adopted by common Roman soldiers in Roman Britain and Gaul. Linguists suggest that its meaning derives from roots for "effective" or "powerful," and nothing at all to do with the glorification of self.

Nantosuelta was a Celtic nature goddess of fire, earth, and fertility. She was thought to have been part of the Irish Tuatha Dé Danann, combined with Sucellus and subsequently with Dagda. Some evidence suggests that hers was the name assumed by The Morrígan after a joining of new alliances or a transformation.

Her name literally means, "sun-drenched valley" or "of winding stream."

Ogmios was the Celtic god of persuasiveness. His name remains a cognate with the Irish god Ogma. He is described as an older version of Heracles, the Greek demigod of great strength. Like Heracles, Ogmios wore a lion skin and carried a club and bow. This Celtic god is made unique, though, by the chains that pierce his tongue, from his smiling mouth, back to the ears of his happy followers.

Ritona (also Pritona) was a Celtic goddess of "water crossings" or "fords." Her temples seemed to have more extras than do many of the other gods — like courtyards which could easily have been used for the placement of ritual offerings or the preparation of religious banquets. Another such temple even had a theater, supposedly for religious performances.

Rosmerta was a Celtic goddess of abundance and fertility. Quite often, her image was found alongside the Roman god Mercury as if she were his consort. She was worshipped from central France to western Germany.

Segomo was a Celtic war god whose name meant "mighty one" or "victor." Naturally, he was associated with the Roman god, Mars, but also with Hercules.

Sirona was a Celtic goddess venerated throughout Gaul, but also worshipped as far east as the Danube River. She has been associated with the Roman goddess, Diana.

Sucellus was a Celtic god frequently depicted with Nantosuelta. He is usually seen carrying a large hammer or mallet, which could easily have been a beer barrel on a long pole.

Suleviae was a group of Celtic goddesses whose name meant "those who govern well." This group was sometimes associated with the Matres. In fact, one inscription starts out, "To the Sulevi mothers…"

Taranis was a Celtic god of thunder. One curious coincidence ties Taranis with the Greek cyclops Brontes (whose name meant "thunder"), because both were associated with a wheel. Some scholars suggest that Taranis was not so much a god of thunder as he was actually thunder itself. His worship spanned a broad territory including Gaul, Britain, parts of former Yugoslavia, and modern Germany. Lucan, the Roman poet, called Taranis a "savage god" who required human sacrifice. Taranis also remains a cognate with the Irish god Tuirenn. Taranis could also have been part of a triune god, Lugus. Because of his association with thunder or identity as thunder, he was also associated with the

Roman god Jupiter, the Greek god Zeus, and the Norse god Thor.

The name, **Virotutis,** was a Celtic byname given the Roman god Apollo. It meant, "benefactor of humanity." Apollo Virotutis was worshipped just south of Switzerland and in western France.

Visucius was a Celtic god whose name meant "knowledgeable" or "of the ravens." He was usually associated with the Roman god, Mercury, and was worshipped from western Germany to northern Spain.

Celtic and Gallo-Roman Religions

The Romans were no fools when they conquered a people. They knew that those whom they conquered were emotionally attached to their gods and their beliefs. So, the Romans encouraged their new subjects to continue to worship their old gods, while suggesting that the divine Roman names were merely alternatives of the Celtic divine names.

Such an attitude was both political and pragmatic. The Celts got to keep something that did not cost anything to the Roman Republic and later Roman Empire, and Rome acquired subjects who were at least nominally satisfied that they could keep something of their past.

Chapter 3 — Local Irish Celt Gods

Sunlight glistened on the River Erne. From their home on a small island near the head of the river's estuary, Lady Delgnat looked down at her husband's boat as it moved to the main shore. He would be gone for days. Partholón was such a responsible king. He loved his people and frequently traveled amongst their farms and dwellings to ensure they were in good health.

Already she felt lonely. But her mind had been on a solution for weeks. Ever since the royal household had acquired that handsome young servant, Topa, she had been dreaming of the time when her husband would leave.

When she was certain her husband was well on his way, she called for the young servant to perform certain chores in her presence. When he had worked up a sweat from his labors, she called him to come close. She felt a tightness in her back and needed his strong hands to massage the kinks out of her muscles. But soon, she had him doing things only a husband should do.

All the while, Delgnat's faithful dog, head cocked to one side, looked on with a curious expression on its face.

The queen held up her finger to her mouth and looked into the dog's eyes. "Quiet, my little Saimer. You mustn't speak of these things."

Topa felt he had to do as his master's wife had commanded him. Yet he feared for what the master might do.

"Don't worry about him," she said. "He will never find out. When he returns, I will be the loving wife, soothing his tired body — the way you are soothing mine."

"Yes, my lady. Can I do anything else for you?"

"Most certainly, my wonderful young Topa. You can hold me through the night."

"But how will we know when your husband returns?"

"I have the guard ready to alert me the moment they spot his boat approaching our island. You have nothing to worry about."

So, Delgnat and Topa enjoyed each other's company for several weeks. She knew he had never spent more than five weeks away at any one time, but the length of each trip varied. And when the time of her husband's return approached, with each new day, she grew more apprehensive.

To remove the tension from her growing worry, she thought of her husband's ale and how it helped to remove anxieties and inhibitions.

"Topa, my darling," she said as they lay in bed after a particularly energetic morning shared with her, "I think we need a bit more to add to our bliss."

"What would that be, my darling?"

"My husband's ale would be nice."

"But how?"

"I know all about it," she replied. "He uses a special, golden tube to suck out the glorious nectar."

"Lovely! Show me this tube."

Delgnat rose from the bed and crossed the room to a dark cabinet. Within it was the massive jug of her husband's ale. She found the tube and affixed it, then took a deep swig, closing her eyes as she swallowed.

"Here, you try," she said.

Topa took the end of the golden tube and sucked on it until he had the fluid squirting into his mouth. "Oh, my! That is good."

The adulterous couple was careful not to drink too much each day, but the ale helped Delgnat relax so she could enjoy her remaining time with her servant.

On the third day, as they were laying in each other's arms, they heard a loud banging on the royal bedroom door.

"Quickly! Get dressed," she told Topa. Then she pointed to the far corner of the room, where a visitor would not be able to see. "Stand over there."

She put on her robe and quickly strode to the door. When Topa was conveniently hidden, she opened the door enough to see who it was.

Sure enough, it was one of the guards.

"My lady, King Partholón is on his way home. The boat is but 15 minutes away."

"Thank you, Galvyn." She waved toward the far end of the hall in dismissal, and closed the door.

Lady Delgnat turned back to Topa and rushed toward him. "Hold me one more time. Kiss me."

The servant complied.

And then Delgnat stepped back, straightening her robe. "Strip the bed of its sheets. They are to be cleaned. Now, move along. From this moment forth, you are once again a servant of this household."

"Yes, my lady." And Topa did as she instructed.

Another 30 minutes passed before Delgnat heard her husband's footsteps. She opened the door to greet him.

"Welcome home, husband." She kissed him on the cheek and he let out a ragged sigh.

"I'm tired, woman. It was a good trip, but I am glad to be home. Go see to my meal. I'm hungry, but I also need to rest."

She left for the kitchen to supervise the preparation of his meal.

In the meantime, he took off his travel clothes and donned something clean. He would bathe later. He noticed in passing the bed sheets had been removed and thought little of it. Cleaning them was a normal enough event.

Then, he noticed the dark cabinet's door was ajar. He had always closed that door, to keep everything neat and orderly. But had he forgotten? Had he been careless the last time he had partaken of his ale? Or had the dog somehow knocked it open?

He shrugged and padded barefoot across the floor to open the cabinet. A little ale would be so nice after such a long ride home.

He sat cross-legged in front of the cabinet and found the golden tube which made it possible to extract the ale. His wife's dog came close and lay down next to him to watch. As he started to draw the liquid into his mouth, he tasted something else from the tube.

For a moment, he sat there thinking about the aroma that came with the smell of ale. There it was — it tasted like Delgnat's lips. But there was something else there, too. There was another aroma that was less familiar, but not entirely strange.

Two people had been drinking from his ale.

Partholón's eyes went wide! "In my bedroom? My ale?"

He glanced again at the naked bed and in his mind, he could see a picture of his wife in the arms of another.

Again, he placed the golden tube in his mouth, but this time he did not suck. He merely let the fragrances waft into his nose to be sorted and cataloged. And then a face emerged — that of young Topa. He had smelled the servant's breath before when being served at the dinner table.

For a long moment, he sat there feeling numb.

Slowly, he got up, found his boots and put them on. Then he went out into the hall and asked the first guard for the location of Topa the servant.

Down near the river, where the clothes were washed, Topa was talking with the laundry maid. The young man looked up as Partholón approached.

"Good day, my lord," said Topa. His face was stiff, his lips tight around a forced smile.

"Not good," replied Partholón. "You've been spending time in my bed." The accusation was a bold move, he knew, but it exacted a reaction which told him the truth.

Instead of a curious, puzzled look, Topa's eyes went wide, his face lost all its color and he started to shake.

Partholón's face went from stern to that of a sardonic smile. In one quick motion, Partholón reached out with his strong hands and crushed the young man's throat. Then he strode quickly to a nearby guard at the dock and drew his sword. The king then turned back to Topa, who was now goggle-eyed and struggling to breathe. Immediately, the king began hacking at the young servant, driving him down to the ground in a bloody pile of disheveled bones.

Then, the king strode back toward his home, climbing the stairs toward his bedroom. The dog came to greet him and felt the king's boot full force. One quick swing of the sword split the dog's skull and the animal toppled over dead. At the sight of it, the king threw down the sword and clenched both of his fists.

Moments later, Lady Delgnat returned to inform her husband the meal would be ready shortly.

Instead, she saw the dog and grew deathly quiet.

"Yes, your damn dog. Be glad it isn't you laying there."

"Why?" Her voice quaked, but grew in strength. "Why did you need to kill my dog? What did it do to you?"

"Oh, it's not what it did, but what its master did. The bed sheets? The ale? The taste of your lips and Topa's breath?"

Delgnat's eyes went wide. "What did you do?"

"You won't be enjoying his arms anymore."

"You monster!" She started to hit him, but he grabbed her wrists. "Did you kill him, too?"

"You have no remorse for your betrayal?" he asked.

"Betrayal?" She jerked away from him, took two steps back and glared at him, rubbing her wrists where he had held her tight. "Betrayal?

It's all your fault. You were the one who left us alone. It was like leaving honey before a woman. It was like leaving milk before a cat, or edged tools before a craftsman. It was like leaving meat before a hungry child. And you would expect them not to take advantage?"

Partholón merely shook his head and left to find other accommodations for the night.

From that day forth, the island where Partholón lived was called Inis Saimera, after Dalgnat's dog. For the king, the life had been taken from his rule.

Characters and Name Meanings

Delgnat (Partholón's cheating wife; unknown meaning)

Galvyn (male name meaning "sparrow;" Irish Celtic)

Partholón (leader of the second group to land in Ireland; unknown meaning)

Saimer (Lady Delgnat's dog; unknown meaning)

Topa (name of Partholón and Delgnat's servant; unknown meaning)

Ancient Ireland, the Celtic Gods and Other Myths

As we've seen, history knows little of the Gallic Celts, except through the writings of the Greeks and the Romans. Foreign prejudices have likely colored those histories, distorting some things and very possibly leaving out other details that could help us understand the Celts more completely.

A similar influence has colored our understanding of Ancient Ireland and its Celtic roots. That influence was the Christianization of Ireland, starting with Palladius (Patrick the Elder) and others in the early 5th century AD. Christianity's hold on Ireland was essentially complete by late in the 5th century, with the arrival of Pātricius (Saint Patrick).

Christians had, by the 5th century, become highly political and egoistic. Any writings that didn't agree with their interpretation of biblical sources were treated with disdain, if not outright contempt.

So, we learn about the early myths of Celtic gods and beliefs from Christian writers, who might add a note that they had recorded these details, but not because they believed in them.

One source claimed to give us the history of Ireland from the very beginning of sentient contact with that land. The book is called *Lebor Gabála Érenn*. The name translates as, "The Book of the Taking of Ireland." It contains a collection of prose and poetry, including narratives about the long history. The earliest known version comes to us from the 11th century — six centuries after the Christianization of Ireland.

The stories describe six different, main incursions (conquests, settlements) by beings who were either gods or legendary mortals, though a seventh group is frequently discussed (the Fomorians).

The People of Cessair

According to Celtic lore, before the biblical Flood, Cessair, a daughter of a supposed son of Noah named Bith, and his wife Birren, set out on a quest to find a new home. Noah had told Bith and his family to escape the coming Flood by traveling to the far West. So, Bith and his extended family took three ships to Ireland, at the western edge of the world. Two of the ships sank before reaching landfall. Amongst the survivors, there were 50 women and three men. The men were Bith, Fintán mac Bóchra, and Ladra. Cessair was amongst the surviving women. So, the women chose primary husbands, and then shared their husbands with the remaining women equally.

Cessair chose Fintán, Alba chose Ladra, and Bairrfhind chose Bith.

Not long afterward, both Bith and Ladra died. That left Fintán to service 50 women. He could not take the pressure, so he fled, leaving the women all to themselves. When the flood finally came, Fintán was the only one to survive by changing himself into a salmon. Later, he became an eagle, and still later a hawk. He lived for 5,500 years, finally turning back into a man who then told the story of Ireland's long history.

The Fomorians

Though the book does not discuss the arrival of the Fomorians, numerous sources discuss a second group — Muintir Partholóin —fighting the Fomorians and vanquishing them.

The Fomorians are described as a hideous and hostile group of monsters or gods who represented all the harmful aspects of nature. The next to last group of inhabitants — Tuatha Dé Danann — would sometimes intermarry with the Fomorians. They even had children with them. This complex relationship between the monstrous and the sublime has been compared to the relationships between the Norse *jötnar* and the *Vanir* (rustic gods) and even *Aesir* (refined gods).

The earliest named ruler of the Fomorians was named Cichol or Cíocal Gricenchos. His people had arrived in Ireland 111 years after the flood with 600 women and 200 men. The Fomorians were a crude folk and lived for 200 years on fish and birds that they found in the wild.

The Muintir Partholóin

The 9th-century tome, *Historia Brittonum,* describes the people of Partholón (the name of their leader) as the first inhabitants of Ireland — not the second or third.

But the book, *Lebor Gabála Érenn,* says that Partholón's followers brought with them many elements of civilization, including the plow, domesticated animals, skills for house building, and the techniques for brewing. After 10 years of coexistence, Partholón defeated Cichol and his Fomoian people at the Battle of Mag Itha.

While Partholón was visiting his lands, his wife, Delgnat, seduced a servant named Topa. However, when Partholón returned, he learned of the affair and killed Topa and his wife's dog. His wife remained defiant, blaming her own sins on her husband's absence.

The king lived for another 20 years after his defeat of the Fomorians. Partholón's people lived in Ireland for 270 years after the king's death. At that time, 5,000 men and 4,000 women succumbed to a plague. Only one man survived — one of Partholón's nephews named Tuan, son of Starn. Like Fintán of the Cessair, Tuan went through several animal transformations returning to human form as a chieftain's son named Cairell. And like Fintán, Cairell (Tuan) could remember the history of Ireland, including his past life amongst the people of Partholón.

The Muintir Nemid

Another of Partholón's brothers, named Tait, was the great-grandfather of Nemed, who was the next great immigrant to Ireland.

It was said that 44 ships sailed from the Caspian Sea to Ireland (which is impossible, because the Caspian is a landlocked lake or inland sea with no outlets to the oceans of the world). In fact, the Caspian is 28 meters below sea level. If there was a connection, water would be flowing into the Caspian Sea, making it almost impossible to sail out, so long as the water continued to flow in an attempt to reach equilibrium with the greater ocean sea level beyond.

The myth tells us that only one ship arrived in Ireland, with Nemed, his immediate family, and several others on board. During his time, four lakes were said to have burst from the ground — Loch Munremair in Luigne, Loch

Annind, Loch Cál in Uí Nialláin, and Loch Dairbrech in Mide. Nemed's tribe cleared 12 plains, changing the face of Ireland forever: Leccmag and Mag Moda in Munster; Mag Tochair in Tír Eogain; Mag Macha in Airgíalla; Mag Selmne in Dál nAraidi; Mag Cera, Mag Eba, Mag Cuile Tolaid and Mag Luirg in Connacht; Mag Muirthemne in Brega; Mag Seired in Tethbae; and Mag Bernsa in Leinster.

Nemed's people also built two forts — Ráth Chindeich in Uí Nialláin and Ráth Chimbaith in Semne. Incredibly, the four sons of Matan Munremar—Boc, Ruibne, Roboc and Rotan—built Ráth Chindeich in a single day. And for some reason, Nemed killed the boys before the following dawn.

The mysterious Fomorians plagued Nemed and his people. The king fought four battles with them and won each of them.

Ironically, though, Nemed and 3,000 of his people died only nine years after their arrival. How so many people were born and matured in nine years is never explained, but the remaining Muintir Nemid struggled without their leader and were continually oppressed by the Fomorians — the dark gods of pestilence and suffering.

Then, one day, 60,000 of the Muintir Nemid rose up and attacked the Fomorians. Although they won their battle, one of the Fomorians attacked with a tidal wave that killed all but one boat load of Nemed's people. The survivors spread out to other parts of the world, leaving Ireland empty of men for another 200 years.

Fir Bolg

The Muintir Nemid who escaped to Greece became known as the Fir Bolg. The name meant "men of bags", which remains rather enigmatic in origin. Some scholars have attempted to interpret the meaning even more, linking "bag" to belly, bellows, sack or even men "full" and "distended" with the fury of battle.

After moving to Ireland, they were ultimately displaced by the Tuatha Dé Danann. Scholars R. A. Stewart Macalister and John Rhys suggested that the Fir Bolg were really the Fomorians who represented the gods of the dark side of nature, while the Tuath Dé were the gods of "growth and civilization."

The Tuatha Dé Danann

These gods of order brought a civilizing force to Ireland, paving the way for the final inhabitants, the Gaelic Celts — the Milesians.

Their full name meant "the people or tribes of the goddess Danu." Their earlier name, Tuath Dé, simply meant "tribe of the gods."

The Fir Bolg were like the rustic *Vanir* of Norse mythology, and the Tuatha Dé Danann were like the more refined *Aesir* of the same pantheon. As before, the Fomorians were like the *jötnar* — the monstrous giants of Nordic myth, which include the evil Loki and his wolf son, Fenrir.

The Tuath Dé dwelt in the Otherworld — the realm of spirit. Each of their members was depicted as heroes, queens, or kings of the distant past, shrouded in mystery beyond the edge of history.

According to *Lebor Gabála Érenn,* the Tuatha Dé Danann were descendants of Nemed's people. They came to Ireland riding in dark clouds, and landing in the mountains of Ireland. Darkness covered the face of the sun for three days. The Tuath Dé burned their ships so there would be no thought of backing out of their decision to bring order to Ireland.

They fought the Fir Bolg and then the Fomorians. Later, they fought against the final wave of invaders — the Milesians.

The Milesians

The Milesians were Goidelic Celts from the Iberian Peninsula. What's interesting is that one genetic study found the present day Irish have genetic ties to the Basques of northern Spain. Though the Basques were not Celtic, they may have intermarried with the Iberian Celts.

When the Milesians arrived in Ireland, they were confronted by the Tuath Dé. War ensued and many were killed. Finally, both sides agreed to divide Ireland. The Tuatha Dé Danann would take the world below — the Otherworld of spirit — while the Milesians would take the world above — the physical world.

Other Irish Celtic Gods

Unless otherwise stated, the following gods and goddesses were members of the Tuatha Dé Danann.

Eochaid mac Eirc was the last High King of Ireland of the Fir Bolg. He was the first to establish a system of justice, bringing relative peace to the land. Throughout his ten-year rule, it never rained, but instead, there was a soft mist of dew that watered the crops. After each growing season, the harvests were bountiful.

When the Tuatha Dé Danann arrived, their king, Nuada Airgetlám, asked for half of Ireland so they could share the land equally. Naturally, the king of the Fir Bolg refused. So, a battle ensued.

During the fierce fighting, Eochaid was struck with a fearsome thirst and he looked for water with which to quench it. But the Druids of the Tuath Dé used their magic to mask all sources of drinking water. While Eochaid frantically searched for water, the goddess Morrigan found him and killed him.

Nuada Airgetlám had been king of the Tuath Dé for seven years before arriving in Ireland. During battle, though, he lost one of his hands. According to tradition, he could no longer be king, because his body was no longer complete. The Tuatha Dé Danann won the war against the Fir Bolg, and gave them one fourth of Ireland, instead of the original suggestion of half. The new king of the Fir Bolg chose Connacht as their kingdom.

But the new rulers of Ireland needed a new king. To promote peace in the land, they selected a young god named Bres who was half-Fomorian and half-Tuath Dé. They chose him because of his great intellect and beauty.

Bres had been the son of Fomorian Prince Elatha and Tuath Dé goddess Ériu. He had grown up quickly, becoming a mature young man in only seven years. Not only was he made the king, but he also married the daughter of The Dagda — the goddess Brighid.

Despite his great intellect, Bres did not possess great wisdom. He favored the people of his father, a Fomorian. He ordered that the Tuatha Dé Danann work as Fomorian slaves and to pay tribute to his father's people. Naturally, his mother and wife did not like this, and the remainder of the Tuath Dé despised him for this.

Among the injustices, Bres forced Ogma to fetch firewood, the Dagda was made to dig ditches around their forts., Bres also forgot his manners when his subjects came calling upon their king. Whenever the Tuath Dé visited his house, they expected their knives to be greased and their breaths to end up stinking of ale when leaving, but none of this happened.

During his seven years of rule, Nuada worked on getting his hand back. At first, his natural hand was replaced with one of silver. Afterward, a new hand of flesh and blood was grown, making the former king whole again. Happily, the Tuath Dé restored Nuada as king and forced Bres into exile. Nuada ruled successfully for another 20 years.

Bres begged his father to help him reclaim the throne, but Prince Elatha refused, telling his son, "You have no right to get it by injustice when you could not keep it by justice."

Lugh was a young and hard working god who joined the court of King Nuada. Lugh was so industrious and intelligent, Nuada realized the young god would make a far better king. So, Nuada stepped down and gave the throne to Lugh, who was half-brother to The Dagda.

Seeking help from a Fomorian named Balor of the Evil Eye, Bres tried to take back the throne by force, leading to all-out war in the land. During the fighting, Nuada was slain and decapitated by Balor. But Lugh found and killed the Fomorian of the Evil Eye. Late in the war, Lugh found Bres on the battlefield unprotected, and the former High King begged for his life. Lugh promised to spare the young god if he would teach the Tuatha Dé Danann all he knew about agriculture.

Lugh ruled Ireland as High King for a long and prosperous 40 years. During his reign, he had several wives — Buí, Nás, Buach and others. Buach committed adultery with Cermait, one of The Dagda's sons. In a jealous rage, Lugh killed Cermait. In return, Cermait's three sons —Mac Gréine, Mac Cecht and Mac Cuill — killed their king by taking him down to Loch Lugborta and drowning him. The Dagda restored his son, Cermait, with his magic staff.

The Dagda was a father figure amongst the local Irish gods, comparable to Nordic Odin and to the pan-Celtic god, Sucellus. He was not only a chieftain, but also a Druid. He was a god of agriculture and fertility, as well as strength and manliness. He was also associated with wisdom and magic. He exercised control over weather, crops, the seasons, and even time itself. Accordingly, he was said to hold the power over life and death in his hands.

The Dagda was a giant man who usually wore a cloak with a hood. With him, he carried a magic staff called the *lorg mór.* One end of his staff could instantly kill; the other could restore life.

He also carried a magic cauldron which could never be emptied, plus a magic harp with which he could control the emotions of men.

Linguists have suggested his name comes from proto-Celtic roots which mean, "the good god." His common name was Eochaid Ollathair.

After the death of King Lugh, The Dagda took the throne and ruled for 80 long years, making him the longest ruling High King of the Tuath Dé.

Ériu, Banba and **Fódla** were a triumvirate of Irish goddesses whose names were given to the island. The names Banba and Fódla are usually only used in poetry to refer to the land, and Ériu's name is considered the matron goddess of Ireland — Éire, which is the Irish name for their land. Together, the three are considered the goddesses of Irish sovereignty. As we've already seen, Ériu was the mother of Bres — the very unpopular High King of Ireland.

Sionnan and **Boann** gave their names to the rivers Shannon and Boyne. The stories of these two goddesses are also the tales of the rivers themselves and how they were formed. The River Shannon is the longest river in Ireland, dividing the country between East and West, with little more than a couple of dozen crossing points.

In the stories of both goddesses, the women went to a well which they were told to avoid. In the well, they each found the Salmon of Wisdom. After catching and eating the fish, they each became the wisest person of all. In each case, the well burst forth a flood of water which swept the goddess out to sea, ending each of their lives, but spreading the life-affirming magic of water across the land.

The Irish believe water is the source of life. It dissolves the divine power and then transfers that power to the land.

Boann was The Dagda's lover and she bore him a daughter named Brighid.

The goddess **Brighid** has been linked to three Cloughtie wells or springs — sacred places of pilgrimage. She became the wife of Bres.

The Morrígan is a group of three divine sisters — Macha, Babd Catha and Nemain — and was associated with the River Unius. The name "Morrígan" meant "great queen." The three together were sometimes known as "the three Morrigna." In the Ulster Cycle, Morrígan was seen as merely an individual.

Donn is an Irish god of the dead. In modern Irish tradition, the notion of "going to the House of Donn" merely means "to die." The name itself means "the dark one."

When the Milesians were invading Ireland, Donn was amongst them. As they neared the southwest coast, Donn spotted the goddess Ériu just before his own death—drowning from a shipwreck. His body was buried on a rocky island which became known as Tech Duinn ("house of Donn").

Ogma was one of the brothers of The Dagda. His name may have been an alteration of the Gallic god Ogmios.

Ler was a god of the sea. He and Bobd Dearg became rivals for the Tuath Dé throne, after the Milesians had won their battle against the gods. In order to appease Ler, Bobd gave him one of his daughters. She bore him four children. When the wife died unexpectedly, Bobd offered another of his daughters as a second wife, so the children would not be without a mother. But Ler's second wife, Aoife, despised the children and turned them into swans for 900 years.

Chapter 4 — Local Gallic Celt Gods

South of the tiny Republic of Rome, the Celts had invaded, and three Roman legions had been sent to keep the invaders at bay. The year was 349 BC, by our modern reckoning. They carried the standard of Roman consul Lucius Furius Camillus, a relative of the great Marcus Furius Camillus, "Second Founder of Rome." Forty-one years had passed since Brennus had sacked Rome. Camillus was anxious for some payback against these new Celtic invaders.

The last several years had seen a great cooling. The summers were not as warm and the harvests had not been as plentiful, but still, these were times of relative prosperity. The Celts were growing in number and the future of Rome and its allies looked bleak.

As the forces gathered to face each other, a giant Celt, named Turi, stepped away from his fellow countrymen. An awkward, old translator struggling to keep up with the giant Celt.

"Tell them," said Turi, "I want to fight one Roman — their best."

The old man walked several paces ahead of where the giant stood and shouted out his message in the Roman language of Latin.

The news of the challenge quickly spread throughout the Roman legions. One young man of 21, a military tribune named Marcus Valerius, liked the idea of putting down this Gallic Celt, no matter how large he was.

Valerius strode quickly to the tent of Consul Camillus, saluting to the guard as he approached.

"Valerius," said Camillus, "what's this about?"

"Consul, the enemy have sent out a champion. I would like to meet their champion in battle."

"Yes, I've heard. Supposedly he is a giant of a man, a full head taller than you."

Valerius chuckled. "So I hear. And that will only make him slower."

"Don't lose," Camillus said sternly, glaring at the young tribune.

Valerius merely smiled and said, "Of course, sir. I intend to set the tone for the coming battle. My win will make the Celts shake in their boots."

"Good," said Camillus. "Make it so."

Valerius saluted his consul and strode from the tent to the field which separated the two armies. In the distance, beyond the giant, he could see the Celtic enemy staring at him.

Behind him, a host of Roman soldiers gathered to witness the coming fight.

Turi laughed at the approaching Valerius. The old translator started to turn back to the Celtic line, but was stopped by the giant. "Tell him my name and what it means." Then, Turi let go of the old man.

The translator took a step forward and said, "Behold the great Turi whose name means 'bear.' Prepare to die at his hands."

At that, the old man turned and ran for the relative safety of the tree line where the other Celts stood.

When Valerius had approached to within ten paces of Turi, the giant nodded, never taking his eyes off the young Roman soldier. Valerius also nodded and started to circle the giant, sword in one hand, shield in the other.

When the two were only five paces apart, something extraordinary happened. A large raven landed on Valerius' helmet and clawed at the giant.

Both men were immediately startled, but Valerius felt a sudden thrill the gods had sent him this winged helper.

Turi lunged at Valerius, but immediately found the bird pecking at his face. Every time the two men got close, the bird chose to attack the Celt. And each time, the Celt grew more and more agitated that this bird was siding with this urban city dweller.

From amongst the Celtic line, someone yelled, "Cathubodua fights for him!" This was followed by a quiet roar amongst the Celts, for they knew that the battle crow goddess was working against them on this day.

The noise from his fellows distracted Turi and he glanced toward them, leaving open his side for a split second. Valerius struck and the giant became infuriated at his own momentary lapse.

Turi lunged at the Roman, only to find the raven flapping its wings, its talons lifting up to strike at his face, and its sharp beak aiming at the Celt's eyes. The giant backed away and rubbed his face, almost stumbling on the uneven ground.

The bird settled once again on Valerius's helmet and the Roman started to circle once more.

This time, Turi lunged in desperation, feinted a thrust, jumped to the side and swung his sword, barely missing Valerius.

The Roman laughed. Turi shook his head, stunned by the Roman's confidence. Valerius rushed Turi, stopped, stepped to the side and struck the giant's flank, wounding him.

Infuriated, Turi came straight at the Roman and found the raven in his face, blinding him to the Roman's location. A moment later, the bird had returned to the helmet and Valerius had struck yet another blow on the Celt's other side.

By now, Turi had become frantic — even a little insane — that he was losing in such a manner. The goddess was against him and he felt his own life hanging in the balance. He fought down his own terror and struck out once more at the Roman, only to be assaulted yet again by the raven.

Suddenly, Turi stepped back, tripping over a rock and fell with a profound thud to the ground. Valerius lunged forward, striking deep into the giant's abdomen. At that, the raven took flight — its job was done.

Valerius struck again across the man's neck, then hacked at each of the giant's arms. To make certain that the win was final, Valerius began to despoil the corpse, cutting off first an ear, gouging an eye, cutting off a hand.

This enraged the other Celts. They left their line and ran headlong toward Valerius. The Roman troops ran to assist their victor and an all-out battle ensued.

When the fighting was finally over, an exhausted Valerius looked up at the sky, hoping to catch a glimpse of the raven who had helped him that day. Not finding the bird, he looked across the field and spotted one of his men. "Quintus," he said, "this day, I owe my life to that raven."

So, from then on, he was known as Marcus Valerius Corvus — the Roman soldier who'd had the Celtic goddess, Cathubodua, on his side.

Characters

Brennan (unknown meaning) chieftain of the Senones, a Celtic tribe. He beat the Romans at the Battle of Allia (July 18, 390 BC), and conquered the city of Rome in 387 BC, holding most of the city for several months.

Cathubodua (goddess name meaning "battle crow," from a root word meaning "victory").

Lucius Furius Camillus (unknown meaning) of the Roman Patrician gens Furia; a relative of Marcus Furius Camillus (c.446–365 BC).

Marcus Valerius Corvus (c.370–c.270 BC) of the Roman Patrician gens Valeria. He was Roman consul on six separate occasions, and was named dictator twice.

Turi (male name meaning, "bear;" Gallic Celt).

Celtic Gods of Gaul

These are some of the dozens of local Celtic gods of ancient Gaul and the surrounding areas.

Bodua (Roman Victoria; Irish Badb). Like the more broadly worshipped Cathubodua ("battle crow"), her name suggests a strong connection to "fighting" and "victory."

Gobannos (Roman Vulcan; Irish Goibniu). His name suggests that he is the patron of metal smiths of all kinds.

Nemetona (Roman Victoria). Her name means "she of the sacred grove." She was worshipped in northeastern Gaul. In Bath, Britain, she was associated with Gallo-Roman Loucetius Mars. One inscription suggests that Nemetona was associated with the Roman goddess Victoria.

Nodens (Roman Mars, Mercury, Neptune and Silvanus; Irish Nuada) was worshipped in Britain, and possibly Gaul, as a god of the sea, hunting, dogs, and healing.

Poeninus was a mountain god frequently associated with Jupiter — the chief Roman god and divine ruler over the sky. Poeninus was also associated with the Swiss Alps crossing now known as Great St Bernard Pass.

Sequana (Roman-Etruscan Minerva) is associated with the spring source of the River Seine and with water's natural healing powers. A large pot at her temple was discovered to be filled with miniature replicas of body parts, made out of silver and bronze. These were the body parts of the parishioners they wanted to be healed by her.

Chapter 5 — Celtic Sagas: The Cycles

The day had ended and both Queen Medb and her new husband and king, Ailill, were in bed together.

She was somewhat older than he, as she had been a teenage queen to Eochaid Dála when she had taken her older sister's young grandson, Ailill, to raise in her household. When Ailill became a teenager, she took him as her lover. He was a strong and handsome young man. And the three things she liked most about him were that he was without fear, meanness, and jealousy.

With her assistance and encouragement, he had become the chief bodyguard. Her husband ordered Ailill expelled from the kingdom, but Medb had refused to obey. When Eochaid Dála had challenged Ailill to mortal combat, the king lost, paying with his life. That had left Medb free to marry her sister's grandson.

Now, they were husband and wife. And Ailill, being born of royalty, liked to brag about his inherited wealth. As they lay on their pillow, Ailill said, "In truth, woman, she is a well-off woman who is the wife of a nobleman."

"She is indeed," said Medb, "Why do you think so?"

He gave her a wry smile and replied, "I think so, because you are better off today than when I married you."

Medb's head rocked back, her mouth open, but mute, and her brow wrinkled with disagreement. "I was well-off before marrying you. Remember, I shared a throne with three men before you. Conchobar mac Nessa, king of Ulster, Tinni mac Conri—"

"To whom you were never officially married."

Medb nodded and held her finger to Ailill's lips. "—with whom I shared the throne of Connacht, and then Eochaid Dála, my protector after my first husband killed Tinni."

Ailill chuckled and said, "It was wealth that we had not heard of and did not know of, but you were a woman of property and foes from lands next to you were carrying off spoils and booty from you."

Shaking her head, Medb replied, "Not so was I, but my father was in the high-kingship of Ireland, namely Eochaid Feidlech, mac Find meic Findomain meic Findeoin—"

This time, Ailill held his finger to her lips. "Please, I know the lineage. I share some of it."

"And he," Medb continued, holding his finger, then lifting it back to her lips to kiss it, "my father had six daughters: Derbriu, Ethne and Ele, Clothru, Mugain and Medb. I was the noblest and worthiest of them. I was the most generous of them in bounty and the bestowal of gifts. I was best of them in battle and fight and combat. I had fifteen hundred royal mercenaries of the sons of strangers exiled from their own land and as many of the sons of native freemen within the province. And there were ten men for each mercenary of these, and nine men for every mercenary and eight men for every mercenary, and seven for every mercenary, and six for every mercenary, and five for every mercenary, and four for every mercenary and three for every mercenary and two for every mercenary and one mercenary for every mercenary. I had these as my standing household, and for that reason my father gave me one of the provinces of Ireland, namely, the province of Crúachu. amMedb Chrúachna."

"Yes," said Ailill, "I know where we live — Ráth Crúachain, fort and capital of all Connacht."

Medb continued, "Messengers came from Find mac Rosa Rúaid, the King of Leinster, to sue for me, and from Cairbre Nia Fer mac Rosa, the King of Tara, and they came from Conchobor mac Fachtna, the King of Ulster, and they came from Eochu Bec. But I consented not, for I demanded a strange bride-gift such as no woman before me had asked of a man of the men of Ireland, to wit, a husband without meanness, without jealousy and without fear."

Ailill looked back at her with admiration, for he knew he alone was such a man.

"If my husband should be mean, it would not be fitting for us to be together, for I am generous in largesse and the bestowal of gifts and it would be a reproach for my husband that I should be better than he in generosity, but it would be no reproach if we were equally generous provided that both of us were generous. If my husband were timorous, neither would it be fitting for us to be together, for singlehanded I am victorious in battles and contests and combats, and it would be a reproach to my husband that his wife should be more courageous than he, but it is no reproach if they are equally courageous provided that both are courageous. If the man with whom I should be were jealous, neither would it be fitting, for I was never without one lover quickly following in the shadow of another."

Medb reached over and kissed her young husband on the lips. "Now such a husband have I got, even you, Ailill mac Rosa Rúaid of Leinster. You are not niggardly, you are not jealous, you are not inactive. I gave you a contract and a bride-price as befits a woman, namely, the raiment of twelve men, a chariot worth thrice-sevencumala, the breadth of your face in red gold, the weight of your left arm in white bronze. Whoever brings shame and annoyance and confusion on you, you have no claim for compensation of for honor-price for it except what claim I have, for you are a man dependent on a woman's marriage-portion."

"Not so was I" said Ailill, "but I had two brothers, one of them reigning over Tara, the other over Leinster, namely, Find over Leinster and Cairbre over Tara. I left the rule to them because of their seniority but they were no better in bounty and the bestowal of gifts than I. And I heard of no province in Ireland dependent on a woman except this province alone, so I came and assumed the kingship here in virtue of my mother's rights, for Máta Muirisc the daughter of Mága was my mother. And what better queen could I have than you, for you are the daughter of the high-king of Ireland."

"Nevertheless" said Medb, "my property is greater than yours."

"I marvel at that," said Ailill, "for there is none who has greater possessions and riches and wealth than I, and I know that there is not."

Medb shook her head in disbelief. How could her wonderful new husband be so obstinate?

"Sir!" she said sternly, "we shall have to do a counting to verify what you say."

"Until the morrow, my love," replied Ailill, and kissed his wife passionately.

Before the sun had risen, Medb was up and dressed. Ailill gazed at her sleepily. "Come here, woman."

"No," she replied. "We have work to do."

She had all their valuable possessions brought forth to be examined and counted. A scribe was brought in to document the accounting. Then all the sheep were brought to the castle to be counted and assessed for overall value.

From the grazing fields and horse paddocks, all the steeds and mares were brought fourth and counted, then all their great herds of swine, and cattle.

So far, everything had been evenly paired. Both Medb and Ailill were perfectly matched in riches, except in cattle.

"But look," said Medb to her husband, "the fertile bull Finnbhennach used to be mine. He was born into my herd."

"And yet," replied Ailill, "Finnbhennach refused to be owned by a woman. I wonder why." He winked at her.

"Oh!" she threw up her hands and slapped her sides in frustration.

Ailill shook his head and smiled a kind, loving smile for his wife. He put his arms around her shoulders and pulled her close. "I'll tell you what, my love. We will solve this problem. And in our position of power, such solutions shall be easy."

She looked up at him and cocked her brow with a questioning look. "What did you have in mind?"

"Let us call the famed Herald Mac Roth. He should know the land well enough to find a comparable bull. Perhaps—"

"Yes, perhaps," she continued, "we can hire the stud to create a herd to make mine larger and more valuable."

"And nothing would give me greater pleasure, my love."

"Thank you, thank you, my kind dear," she replied, running from him back to the castle to send for the herald.

When Mac Roth had been summoned, he listened to Medb's pleas for help.

"I know indeed," said Mac Roth, "where there is a bull even better and more excellent than he, in the province of Ulster in the cantred of

Cúailnge in the house of Dáire mac Fiachna. Donn Cúailnge is his name."

"Go there, Mac Roth, and ask of Dáire for me a year's loan of Donn Cúailnge. At the year's end, he will get the fee for the bull's loan, namely, fifty heifers, and Donn Cúailnge himself returned. And take another offer with you, Mac Roth: if the people of that land and country object to giving that precious possession, Donn Cúailnge, let Dáire himself come with his bull and he shall have the extent of his own lands in the level plain of Mag Aí and a chariot worth thriceseven cumala, and he shall have my own intimate friendship."

Mac Roth's eyes went wide at this last detail, but he said nothing. Would the queen sleep with Dáire to sweeten the deal?

So, Mac Roth and his entourage traveled over land to the Kingdom of Ulaidh and to the house of Dáire mac Fiachna. A total of nine messengers were welcomed into the cattle baron's home.

Dáire treated his guests like royalty. After all, Mac Roth was the most highly esteemed herald on the island. Anyone would be honored to have this messenger as a guest.

When the lord of the house had heard the complete message, he was as delighted as any man could ever be. "By the truth of my conscience, even if the Ulstermen object, this precious possession, Donn Cúailnge, will now be taken to Ailill and Medb in the land of Connacht."

Mac Roth and the other messengers were incredibly pleased to hear of Dáire's favorable answer.

To rejoice in his own good fortune, Dáire bade his guests stay for a feast to celebrate.

But well into the celebration, the other messengers began to talk amongst themselves about details that had not been discussed with Dáire — that were, in fact, not true. Some of them talked about the generosity of the various lords and landowners. And finally, one of them said, "I should like to see a gush of blood and gore from the mouth from which that talk comes, for if the bull were not given willingly, he would be given perforce."

In other words, the messenger implied that if Dáire were not agreeable, then Medb and Ailill would have come and take the bull by force.

So drunk were the messengers they didn't notice the lord's butler and junior servant arrive with more food and ale. The butler heard that last remark. He put down the platter of food, and nodded harshly for the servant to deposit the ale, and they left in a hurry.

The butler returned to the main house and went straight to his master. "My lord, the messengers just revealed a most disturbing truth —if you had not agreed to the terms, the king and queen of Connacht would have come to take your bull by force."

"What?" asked Dáire. "This is outrageous. I swear by the gods whom I worship unless they take him thus by force, they shall not take him by fair means."

In the morning, the messengers went back to the lord's house. Mac Roth said, "Guide us, noble sir, to the spot where Donn Cúailnge is."

"Not so, indeed," said Dáire, "but if it were my custom to deal treacherously with messengers, travelers or voyagers, not one of you should escape alive."

"What is this?" said Mac Roth.

"There is great cause for it," said Dáire. "You said that if I did not give the bull willingly, then I should give him under compulsion by reason of the army of Ailill and Medb and the sure guidance of Fergus."

"Nay," said Mac Roth, "whatever messengers might say as a result of indulging in your meat and drink, it should not be heeded or noticed nor accounted as a reproach to Ailill and Medb."

"Yet, I shall not give my bull, Mac Roth, on this occasion."

And so began the Great Táin Bó Cúailnge — the Great Cattle Raid of Cooley.

Characters and Name Meanings

Ailill (male name meaning "elf") was the mythical king of Irish Connaught, in west central Ireland. His full name was Ailill mac Máta, the surname being matronymic after his mother.

Dáire (male name meaning "fruitful," "fertile" and "rage") was the mythical lord and owner of Donn Cúailnge, living in northeastern Ireland in a region known as Ulaidh (part of modern Ulster).

Donn Cúailnge ("donn" means "the dark one;" Cúailnge is an area of the north of Ireland now known as Cooley) was a powerfully fertile stud bull, owned by Dáire mac Fiachna. He was the object of the cattle raid (Táin bo) of Cooley.

Mac Roth (male name meaning "son" of Roth, which may mean "red," "wood" or "fame") was a highly respected messenger.

Medb (female name meaning "intoxicating") was Ailill's queen. She took many lovers and had many kings to serve on the Connaught throne with her.

The Mythological Cycle

The Mythological Cycle includes several stories about the divine beings who arrived in Ireland during the five invasions. Most of the focus is on the Tuatha Dé Danann. These are the groups we talked about in the chapter on Irish Celtic gods.

The Ulster Cycle

The Ulster Cycle is a collection of stories centered on the rule of King Conchobar mac Nessa of Ulaidh (an ancient name for Ulster). Within the numerous tales, the most significant hero is the king's nephew, Cú Chulainn.

The primary source of conflict in the tales was the Connachta, led by Queen Medb and her husband, Ailill. Medb's chief ally in these disputes was the former king of Ulaid, Fergus mac Róich, now in exile from his home. We've already seen a small part of the most extensive story within the cycle — the "Cattle Raid of Cooley," also known as Táin Bó Cúailnge.

Queen Medb raised a massive army to steal the nation's prize bull, and the only one defending the creature was Cú Chulainn, the king's nephew.

One of the best-known stories concerns the tragedy of Deirdre, which has been used by others as inspiration for their works, most notably, by J.M. Synge and W.B. Yeats.

The Cycle also includes numerous stories of courtships, birth, deaths, and of the many conflicts between the characters.

In the Ulster Cycle, The Morrígan ("great queen") finds her first mention. Here, she was a single goddess, instead of three. In the Ulster Cycle, she had a conflicted relationship with the hero, sometimes supporting him, sometimes taunting him, and at other times attempting to destroy his chances at success.

The Fenian Cycle

The Fenian Cycle is also called the Fiannaíocht and sometimes even the Ossianic Cycle, named after Oisín, the cycle's narrator.

The focus of this Cycle was the adventures of Fionn mac Cumhaill, a mythical hero. This Cycle also dealt with Fionn's warriors, known as the Fianna.

Sequentially, this is the third Cycle, after the Ulster and before the Historical.

Some of the various tales also involve individual Fianna warriors, like Caílte, Diarmuid and Oisín's son Oscar. It also includes stories of Fionn's chief adversary, Goll mac Morna.

In the Cycle, the Fianna warriors were brought together by High King Cormac mac Art as guardians of the kingdom. Membership in the Fianna was dominated by Cumhal's Clan Bascna and Goll's Clan Morna.

Years earlier, the Morna had killed Cumhal, leader of Clan Bascna, after the Battle of Knock. Someone also stole Clan Bascna's treasure bag. Muirne, Cumhal's wife, whom he had kidnapped to force her marriage, escaped, though she was already pregnant by her now dead husband.

Muirne's father refused to take her back, because of a prophecy which had foretold of his own demise stemming from her marriage. Instead, he ordered her to be burned, but the High King protected her, and placed her in the care of a woman named Bodhmall and a woman warrior named Liath Luachra. When she finally gave birth to a boy, she named him Deimne. Later, however, her son became known as Fionn mac Cumhaill, the future leader of the Fianna.

The Cycles of the Kings

The Cycles of the Kings is also known as the Historical Cycle. The word "cycles" is more appropriate, because there are a number of independent groups of tales involved. Naturally, these groupings contain tales of the legendary rulers of the island, like Niall of the Nine Hostages, Lóegaire mac Néill, Conall Corc, Cormac mac Airt, Diarmait mac Cerbaill, Éogan Mór, Conn of the Hundred Battles, Brian Bóruma, Lugaid mac Con, Crimthann mac Fidaig, and Guaire Aidne mac Colmáin.

The bards of medieval Ireland (court poets) were tasked with recording the lineage and history of their king. Their poetry combined both historical facts and fanciful mythology. The amount of each — fact and mythology — varied from bard to bard, but the results were invariably a skillful packaging of the "brand" that was their king and his family. It was an early form of advertising, meant to impress other families and other nations.

The earliest king in these Cycles was the High King Labraid Loingsech who supposedly rose to the throne in 431 BC. Was he a real person, or merely some fanciful invention of one of the bards? We don't know. But the Cycles include many well-documented rulers who are known truly to have lived, though some of the details might be a bit questionable.

Perhaps the most celebrated tale of this Historical Cycle or Cycles is called the Buile Shuibhne (translated as "The Frenzy of Sweeney").

As king of Dál nAraidi, Suibhne had been cursed by Saint Ronan to become a hybrid being — half-bird, half-man. He had been damned to spend the remainder of his existence in the woods fleeing from humans.

Chapter 6 — Celtic Beliefs: Animal and Human Sacrifice

By the grace of the gods, evening had interrupted the battle. It had become too dark to fight. This blessed fact had become horribly apparent when men had begun to hack at their own friends, rather than at the enemy.

Lord Karney led his men back to their camp from the battlefield. He was as weary as every other man fighting under him, except perhaps the wounded, of which there were many. Nearly everyone helped carry the wounded. And despite being exhausted from battle, they each helped to dress the wounds of those who had been injured.

As everyone helped with tending to the wounded, the staff of the camp prepared the evening meal. These tired warriors needed nourishment so their weary muscles could be rejuvenated, or their wounds could be healed. Karney looked over the mass of bodies going about their various tasks. A deep sadness crossed his mind and weighed heavily on his expression.

Commander Glifieu noticed his king's dour face and asked, "What is it, my lord?"

"You need to ask?" Karney shook his head. "We're losing. I doubt we'll survive the morrow."

"Then we will die bravely, my lord, doing what we must to protect our people."

Karney snorted half a laugh, dry and without humor. "Protect? More like failing to protect."

Glifieu's expression also became glum. "What can we do, sire?"

The look on Karney's face stiffened and he squinted, not looking at anything in particular. For a moment, he was deep in thought. Then he turned to his commander. "Call all your officers together." Karney nodded sharply, and Glifieu turned and started rounding up all the officers.

When they were assembled, Karney stood before them with his hands on his hips. He walked up and down the line of them, inspecting the looks on their faces and the posture of their bodies. They were all good men — strong and faithful. These men were worth dying for.

"My brothers," Karney said finally. "The gods require death so that others may live. Very much as in the hunt, when we ask the gods' permission to slaughter a deer or a boar — or even to catch a fish. Now, we are losing. Can we change that? Can we ask — even plead with the gods? If they demand life for life, then perhaps it is time for the ultimate sacrifice so that our people may survive this tragedy."

"But, my lord," said Nels, one of the lieutenants, "if we're losing, we will all be dead soon enough. How will that help?"

Pwyll, an older captain, snorted and spoke up, "He's young, my lord." He then laughed and shook his head. "Forgive his ignorance. I volunteer for the sacrifice. I've seen better days and my fighting skills are not what they used to be."

Karney shook his head. "But will it be enough? I don't think so. I feel certain that the gods require something bigger and more important. I am the one who needs to volunteer. As we entered the camp this evening, I spoke briefly with one of the Druids and he agrees with me. We need a far larger sacrifice if our people are to escape the ultimate tragedy."

There was a sudden clamor of voices throughout the camp. Everyone heard what had been said. Even the weakest of the wounded turned toward their king, ears bristling to hear more.

"No, my lord," said Pwyll. "We need our leader. You have a wisdom many of us can't touch, and which all of us cannot equal. We need your guidance for when the war is over."

"But," said Karney, "we need to remain alive. I will be born again. I'm not concerned about that. We need life so any wisdom will have a purpose. And we can have faith the gods will deliver a new source of wisdom to us."

"No, my lord," said Kirwyn, a captain who had been wounded severely enough to be laying down nearby, recuperating. "I have been wounded and I'm not certain I will survive. And most assuredly, I will not be of much use to any of us in tomorrow's battle. Please, let me, and any other of the wounded who volunteer, be the gift required by the gods. We will all come back as better warriors in the next life."

"Yes, please let us do this thing," said another of the wounded.

And a host of voices rose up with "Yes!" and with other words of affirmation.

Karney blinked several times to keep the wetness in his eyes from showing. He swallowed with difficulty and nodded slowly. "Very well. Let it be done. Who will volunteer?"

Without exception, every seriously wounded warrior gave some sign of assent. Those who could walk, came forward to the Druids to perform the sacred ceremony, so the gift would be properly received by the gods. Those who were too weak had others help them forward.

And before the night was full, 384 men had given their lives so that the tribe might vanquish their enemy in the coming battle.

Characters and Name Meanings

Glifieu (male name meaning, "mythical son of Taran;" Celtic).

Karney (male name meaning, "fighter;" Celtic).

Kirwyn (male name meaning, "dark skinned;" Celtic).

Nels (male name meaning, "chief;" Celtic).

Pwyll (male name meaning, "mythical lord of Annwn;" Celtic).

Sacrifice

Did the Celts perform animal sacrifices? Like many animist societies, they felt killing any creature was an act that needed to be sanctified — to make the killing less selfish, an act which the gods and nature might deem necessary for the continuation of life.

Animal sacrifice was quite common in the ancient world. Even the Romans performed animal sacrifice, making each such event an elaborate affair. But we know the religious and cultural behavior of the Celts largely from the writings of their enemies — the Romans, Greeks and others. For instance, Lucan, the Roman poet, called Taranis a brutal deity who required human sacrifice.

Cultures have long demonized their enemies to justify their own brutal treatment and attacks on those cultures. Such behavior has been quite common throughout ancient times and even into modern times. If a military leader wanted his men to attack another group, naturally he wouldn't use sweet words to describe their enemy.

Archaeologists have found evidence in Gordion, Anatolia (modern Turkey) which suggests some human sacrifice was performed. Before we look at the evidence, let us look at the historical back story.

After Alexander the Great (356–323 BC) had conquered much of the known world, his empire was divided amongst his men. Around 280 BC, a large army of Celts attacked Macedonia, Alexander's homeland. Two years later, King Nicomedes I of Bithynia welcomed 20,000 Celts as allies. They called themselves Galatai and they migrated from northwestern Anatolia, where the Turkish peninsula faces Europe. They ended up settling in central Anatolia, bringing with them 2,000 wagons filled with baggage, plus 10,000 additional people, including wives, children, merchants and others. These Galatians settled in Gordion. Later, the Romans would call that region "Galatia."

In the last few decades of excavation at Gordion, scientists have uncovered two sites where human bones were piled on top of one another. Each skeleton had suffered a broken neck. According to Greco-Roman sources, Celtic Druids (religious leaders) would sometimes sacrifice humans to forecast the future. Such sacrifices may have been performed on prisoners of war or criminals.

Celts typically cremated their dead, collecting their bones and ashes in perishable containers such as leather bags, wooden barrels, or wicker baskets. Finding piles of bones not collected in the normal burial fashion proved to be quite startling to the archaeologists investigating the Gordion site.

In attempting to explain the behavior of human sacrifice, the first century BC historian Diodorus Siculus presented the idea that human sacrifice was merely a bargaining strategy. Whether Siculus interviewed Celts or merely made up his analysis as a logical idea, we do not know. Siculus suggested the gods or demons demanded a life, so the Celts offered lives to save lives. If some were afflicted with disease, then humans would be sacrificed to prevent the disease from spreading to others. Such appeasement, they supposedly hoped would placate the gods and their desire for death. In battle, the wounded might sacrifice themselves to buy the lives of those who were yet uninjured. Sometimes, a great leader may even sacrifice himself so the battle might turn in their favor.

Captives from a battle were never held for ransom by the Celts, but were sacrificed to fulfill oaths given during battle. Victims were sacrificed in various manners depending on the god which the Celts wanted to appease. For instance, victims of human sacrifice might be burnt alive to placate Taranis. For Teutates, a victim might be suffocated. For Esus, the tree god, death might be by hanging from a tree. Drowning might be employed to satisfy any of the local water deities.

Victims of human sacrifice may have been captives, the ill, criminals who had been imprisoned, or perhaps even members in good standing within their own tribe. The Roman senator and historian, Tacitus stated, "the Druids consult the gods in the palpitating entrails of men." Disemboweling a man or woman and examining the shape of their entrails would somehow help the religious priest discover the future. Though the Romans did not perform human sacrifice, they did use the entrails of birds to understand the best course of action.

The Greek geographer and historian, Strabo, wrote that Druid priests would strike down a sacrificial victim to study how their body convulsed before death. Such convulsions would tell them what they needed to know from the gods.

The Wicker Man

We have two Roman sources — Julius Caesar and Strabo the geographer — who describe the Wicker Man. According to them, a huge, wicker statue of a man was sometimes created by the Celts. Within the torso of the statue, there was room enough to hold a man or woman—the object of a human sacrifice. Once the victim was placed inside, a ceremony might be performed and the Wicker Man would be set ablaze.

Though there is insufficient archaeological evidence to corroborate their story, we must remember that a lack of evidence never disproves a thesis, either. Any stronger claims, one way or the other, are logically fallacious without more evidence.

We know that people in power have used negative stereotypes to demonize their enemies. That's part of human nature — the selfishness to get ahead, so this is certainly a possibility, but not one that has been proven. It's a clever idea, but there is no proof that either Julius Caesar or Strabo used such a deceitful trick on this topic.

Such Wicker Men would be used by Druids to burn prisoners or criminals as a tribute to the Celtic gods. When no criminals could be found, the Druids would sometimes use slaves instead.

But until we have more solid evidence, if ever, we must remain uncertain about the validity, or historical accuracy of this Wicker Man phenomenon.

Chapter 7 — Celtic Beliefs: Reincarnation

Vercingetorix stood before his commanders and their staff, surveying their mood.

"We have a supreme advantage over these Latins. They fear death, thinking that it is the end of all things. Fear can strengthen a man's efforts, but more often, it can also distract and befuddle."

A rumble of affirmations ran through the crowd of warriors.

"These Latins think they have an advantage over us. And they do. So long as we remain separate, we will not be strong enough to win against them, despite their fear of death. But with our combined forces, working together, and fearless of death, we shall crush these invaders and oppressors."

Cheering erupted amongst the men. Vercingetorix allowed it to die down naturally.

"We know," continued the leader, "that memory rarely travels with us from one life to the next, but we are confident of the transference. Many of us can feel the depth of our spiritual existence, even if we don't have all the details. But some of us have remembered. Some of us have called out the names of loved ones still alive and have even remembered their nicknames and other details that confirm their identity as a reincarnated friend."

More noises of affirmation rumbled through the assembly.

"When we dispatch our brethren to the otherworld, we do so not so much in malice because they oppose us and want to kill or enslave us, but for the balance of things, so that nature remains protected from those who would despoil her. We know that they are not hurt by their death, because it is no more than the removal of one cloak, awaiting the next."

"But they know," said one of the other chieftains. "Their leader, Julius Caesar, he already knows of our beliefs. Would that knowledge work against us?"

Vercingetorix blinked, then glared at the man. What a fool, he thought. Here I am, attempting to bolster the spirits of our men, and he trashes everything I've said. He nodded slowly, his mind racing to come up with a powerful response. He hoped what he said next would restore the bond of strength he had attempted to forge.

"That is true, my friend," and he scanned the remaining chieftains, their generals and staff, "but it is one thing to hear about such things and to disbelieve them, and it is entirely different to live such beliefs and to know their validity in your very bones."

Everyone in the hall cheered exuberantly. Even the one doubtful chieftain saw the wisdom in it.

"This Julius Caesar is clever as a fox," continued Vercingetorix. "But we have other advantages. "We have our food stores. His men will have to scavenge for food. We know the land better than he does. But don't ever let these things blind us to the very real danger. He could still win. He has technology that is new to us. We've seen it work and our artisans still don't know how to build such things, like their—" he hesitated, searching for the word.

"Siege weapons, my lord," said someone nearby.

"Yes, siege weapons. So, we will have to be even more clever and ferocious. We need to use nature to our advantage; the gods be willing."

Again, he surveyed the group, assessing their mood. It seemed somewhat improved.

"We can still win this, my friends. Let us work together as well as we work with nature. Let our own individual selfishness for domination be subdued, just as we subdue our own egos when going on the hunt—asking the gods for permission. Let us gain each other's permission to allow this union to work."

Again, there were cheers, and Vercingetorix let out a loud whoop! Others picked up on the noise and repeated it, turning it into a chant.

The leader let the noise go on for a minute, then waved his arms over his head. "Okay, okay, my friends. Let us do this."

Our One Character and Name Meaning

Vercingetorix (male name meaning, "king over warriors;" ancient Gallic Celt). This was the name of the king of the Arverni tribe who united many of the Gauls against Julius Caesar. In the end, he was defeated, transported to Rome and then executed.

A Belief in Reincarnation

Most Christians think of reincarnation as an Eastern idea, but it remained quite common throughout the world, including amongst the ancient Greeks, Celts, Jews (especially the Kabbalists), and even the early Christians.

Julius Caesar, when writing about his campaigns against the Celts of Gaul, said, "A lesson which [the Druids] take particular pains to inculcate is that the spirit/mind does not perish, but after death passes from one body to another; they think this is the best incentive to bravery, because it teaches men to disregard the terrors of death" — De bellico Gallico VI, 14.

Another chronicler from the same period wrote, "The Pythagorean doctrine prevails among the Gauls' teaching that the consciousness/souls of men are immortal, and that after a fixed number of years they will enter into another body" — Alexander Cornelius Polyhistor, 1st century BC.

Jarnail Singh quotes Julius Caesar in his book, "With regard to their actual course of studies, the main object of all education is, in their opinion, to imbue their scholars with a firm belief in the indestructibility of the human soul, which, according to their belief, merely passes at death from one tenement to another; for by such doctrine alone, they say, which robs death of all its terrors, can the highest form of human courage be developed" Druids in World Religions and the New Era of Science, p. 172.

With reincarnation, there is the promise of continued life, even without the continuity of memory. But the Celts were already familiar with the need for humility. Their prayers and rituals spoke of this need, lest they anger the gods and lose the opportunity to find the food and other resources needed for their survival.

Chapter 8 — Celtic Beliefs: Matriarchy

Keelia sat at the place of prominence within the great lodge house. Her husband, Naois, sat on a lower step, looking over the throng of visitors.

Royal Prince Naois stroked his graying beard and looked back to his wife. After all these years, she still looked beautiful, and he was certain it wasn't merely his own prejudice. Queen Keelia could feel her husband staring at her, but she would not give in to the temptations of personal desire while presiding over the council of the tribes.

"Who is next?" asked Keelia, raising her right arm toward the crowd.

"I am, my lady." A tall and somewhat muscular woman strode toward the center of the lodge house.

"Yes, Joyce. What do you require of me, today?"

"Permission, my lady." The woman hesitated and looked at some of the others on the side of the mass of people in attendance. "We have grown prosperous over the last few generations. Our numbers are now too great for this small valley. I recommend that we send some of our number to the West in order to find another suitable home."

Keelia offered half a laugh and nodded. "I've been thinking the same thing, good lady." She stood and turned from one side of the lodge house to the other, surveying all in attendance. "I nominate Joyce to be the leader of our new tribe. Any who would like to go with her are welcome, but to be limited to five hundred. That should be enough to get your new tribe started. After one year, you are to send a messenger back here to report on your progress. At that time, I will judge whether others may go to join you. Are there any objections?"

Joyce was noticeably shaken by the sudden approval. And no one spoke out against her nomination.

"Very well," said Keelia. "You are to take the first 500 volunteers, starting early tomorrow morning. And you shall have everything you may require."

"Thank you, my lady." Joyce bowed slightly and backed away, smiling broadly.

"Very well," replied Keelia. "And who is next?"

An older man, holding a hat in his hands, shuffled forward and bobbed his head several times. His hands fidgeted with the hat, rotating it nervously.

"Gwawl, isn't it?" asked Keelia.

"Yes, my lady," he replied and merely stood there, furtively glancing at his monarch.

"I would like to give you all the time you need," said Keelia, "but I do have other responsibilities. Can you speak?"

"Yes, yes, my lady. I — er."

Queen Keelia shook her head, blinked and took a deep breath. "I won't bite you, my good man. Out with it, or hold your peace."

Suddenly, Gwawl blurted out everything he had to say in one dense string of words. "So many other cultures surrounding us have male leaders and they jeer at us for having a woman in the ruling seat."

Keelia's face went slack, her head trembling as if slapped.

The old man took a step backward. His head turned slightly as if eyeing the path for a quick escape.

"Perhaps I was wrong," said Keelia, "to say that I wouldn't bite."

Everyone in the lodge suddenly roared with laughter. The queen also laughed softly and squinted at the old man. "So, are you here to claim the throne?"

More laughter, but it quickly died down on its own accord.

"No, no, no, my lady." Gwawl looked nervously from one nobleman to the next. "It's just that perhaps the next ruler should be a man."

"And does anyone else, here, feel the need to bow to this ridicule from other tribes?"

Everyone grew silent.

"Does anyone think that a woman ruling makes us weaker?"

"No, my lady," said one of the elders. "A man might do as good a job, but he could also do worse. We have beat many invaders. Their words are empty."

Queen Keelia nodded, but there was no enthusiasm in the gesture. "Very well. I will consider these things. That is all for now." She lifted her hand and waved at the crowd in dismissal.

When all were gone but the honor guard and her husband, she took his hand and led him out of the lodge house toward a nearby meadow. In the distance, she could see the northern Alps rising above the forested hills. The land was rich with life and abundance. The mid-afternoon sun made all the summer green glisten.

"What do you think of this idea?" Keelia asked her husband.

Naois tilted his head back and breathed deeply the clean forest air. Then, he lifted Keelia's hand to his lips and kiss it. "I have always trusted your judgment, my love. But this is not the first time we have heard of this attitude of the patriarchal tribes. We value both genders. In their tribes, women are little more than slaves. I wouldn't want that. And I'm happy to have far more freedom than they give their women."

"I don't think we could lose our love for one another so easily," said Keelia. "If you were to become king, I suspect that everything would be very much the same as before. Except—" she chuckled softly, "I might have more rest, not being so put upon by the responsibilities of the people."

For several minutes, they merely held each other. Finally, a breeze kissed their cheeks, and they stepped apart.

Still holding hands, they made their way back to their encampment.

"I will give this much thought," said Keelia. "I would not want the patriarchal tribes to attack us simply because they think we are weak. That could become tiresome. But so far, that has not been a problem."

Characters and Name Meanings

Gwawl (male name meaning "mythical son of Clud;" Celtic).

Joyce (female for Jodoc, a male Celtic name meaning "lord").

Keelia (female name meaning "slender of comely;" Celtic).

Naois (male name meaning "mythical warrior;" Celtic).

Where Women Ruled

Suleviae was a group of Celtic goddesses whose name meant "those who govern well." This group was sometimes associated with the Matres (mothers). In fact, one inscription starts out, "To the Sulevi mothers..."

The fact that the Matres and Matronae were a primary, divine trinity suggests that females were held in higher regard throughout Celtic society.

The fact that Boudicca went to war with the Romans to protect her daughters' birthrights shows that women were more highly respected in their society and had more rights.

Both Romans and Greeks greatly despised the Etruscans (northern Italy) for the power they gave their women, so we know the prejudice in those two societies ran deep against any concept of female empowerment. And since we receive most of our knowledge of Celtic culture from Greco-Roman sources, it's easy to understand how something like a matriarchal society would be dismissed, suppressed, or even willfully forgotten.

Modern scholars consider the Picts of Scotland to be ethnolinguistically Celtic in origin. And some scholars feel the Picts were a matriarchal society. Even more scholars acknowledge the possibility the Picts were a matrilineal society, where men ruled, but only by marrying the daughter of an earlier king. So, whoever married the princess would become the king.

Because the Romans could never conquer the Picts, those invaders built Hadrian's Wall at the north end of England to keep the Picts from roaming too far south. But there was little contact with the Picts, so we know very little about them, especially because there was no writing amongst them.

Most assuredly, the Celts were patriarchal in the historical periods of the Iron Age. But we know almost nothing of the Celts before 500 BC.

There is evidence that some other cultures were matriarchal at some prehistoric point in the past, but we do not know what could have caused the switch or how it progressed across the Eurasian landscape, if indeed it did happen at all.

Even though we don't have direct evidence of explicit matriarchy, we do have evidence of a more egalitarian society. The Celts viewed women differently than their Roman and Greek neighbors. They had women rulers and warriors, like Medb, who, as we've seen, took many lovers and had many kings to serve on the Connaught throne with her.

We also learned about Medb's traits from her conversation with her husband in the story of the Cattle Raid of Cooley in the Ulster Cycle. "But my father was in the high-kingship of Ireland [and] had six daughters: Derbriu, Ethne and Ele, Clothru, Mugain and Medb. I was the noblest and worthiest of them. I was the most generous of them in bounty and the bestowal of gifts. I was best of them in battle and fight and combat. I had fifteen hundred royal mercenaries of the sons of strangers exiled from their own land and as many of the sons of native freemen within the province."

Romans would likely choke on this statement of female power. Indeed, they tried to cheat Boudicca's daughters out of their inheritance, and that led to the sacking of the young settlement that would one day become the great city of London.

We also know the names of men sometimes included a matronymic — such as that of Medb's husband, Ailill mac Máta's — "mac Máta" coming from his mother.

And we know some of the chief divinities of the Celtic pantheon were female. All these clues open the door to the notion the Celts may at one time have been a matriarchy.

Conclusion – What We Have Learned

We gained a healthy perspective on the Celts and how they fit into our shared history and heritage. Their culture stretched across nearly all of mid-latitude Europe and partly into Asia — from Ireland to Anatolia.

The mild climate of the mid-Holocene helped the Celts grow their numbers in central Europe, expanding into an ever-broader territory. As the Celts reached their greatest numbers, the Romans were on the verge of their own initial expansion.

We got a taste of the Celtic reverence for nature, how they viewed the physical properties of their environment as imbued with spirit. We compared their early animism with the more structured polytheism of the Etruscans, Romans and the Greeks.

Chapter 2 gave us a look at many of the Celtic gods that were worshipped across a broad territory. We also learned how many of the Celtic gods became generally mixed with the Roman pantheon and the two cultures — conqueror and conquered — became as one. We learned of individual Celtic gods, and learned some of the little we do know about their traits — gods like Epona, Matres and

Matronae, Toutatis, Belenus, Cathubodua, Cernunnos, Esus, Lugus, Ogmios and Taranis.

In chapter 3, we settled into the deeply mythological tales of Ancient Ireland, and the several invasions of the god-kings who first migrated to the Emerald Island.

Chapter 4 took us back to the continent and the Celts of Gaul, learning more about their local gods. We even saw how one Roman officer might have gotten a surprising taste of Celtic divine help.

In Chapter 5, we discovered about the Celtic Sagas and the four main Cycles — The Mythological Cycle, The Ulster Cycle, The Fenian Cycle and the Cycles of the Kings.

Celtic beliefs gave us the subjects of the last few chapters, with chapter 6 covering animal and human sacrifice. We gained a better understanding of how the Celts may have justified such societal behavior, because of their unique views of life, balance with nature and the gods, and their belief in reincarnation. We also learned a little about the phenomenon of The Wicker Man.

The concept of reincarnation, in chapter 7, helped us see how the Celts could be so fearless in battle.

And finally, in the last chapter, we saw how the possibility of a matriarchal past, where women ruled instead of men, may have given the Celts a far more egalitarian society.

Can you help me?

If you enjoyed this book, then I'd really appreciate it if you would post a short review on Amazon. I read all the reviews myself so that I can continue to provide books that people want.

Thanks for your support!

Preview of Norse Mythology
A Fascinating Guide to Understanding the Sagas, Gods, Heroes, and Beliefs of the Vikings

Introduction—Climate Change Made Them Ruthless

The Vikings of Norse poetry and saga were a fearless lot, and their tales were frequently tragic. Some, if not all, of the myths were based on real people and real events. These heroes accomplished many fantastic feats, some of them even documented by their enemies.

The Vikings were born out of an age of hardship. Tales of their earliest raids come to us from the 790s, during the early European Middle Ages. This was a period of dangerous iciness as the thousand-year climate cycle dipped to the coldest our world had experienced in 7,000 years. No doubt, the punishing cold for these people of Northern Europe helped to dispel any complacency they may have felt during the warmer, mid-Holocene epoch. Death was sitting on their doorstep and the weak and timid would have died from the change in climate. Only the strong and cunning would survive.

The Vikings began to raid villages farther south, conquering parts of what is modern day Netherlands, France, England and Ireland. The Vikings also became adventurers and traders, taking their wares as far as Byzantium, Baghdad and Kiev.

Generally speaking, the Norwegian clans spread throughout the western portions of Europe—Scotland, Iceland, and even into the Americas in Greenland and Canada's Newfoundland. The Danes attacked and settled in England and France's Normandy. In fact, the Normans who later conquered Anglo-Saxon England and who became the British aristocracy were originally of Viking blood. The Swedes traveled East and established the Kievan Rus' in what is today the Ukraine. And these Norsemen even ruled over the southern Mediterranean island of Sicily. But even these rules of thumb do not cover all of Norse history. Some Norwegians also traveled to the Slavic lands of East Europe.

So fierce were the Norse warriors that the kings of the Byzantine Empire kept some of them as their Varangian Guard to protect the royal household.

Though there were regional distinctions in language and culture, the modern nations of Denmark, Sweden and Norway would not exist for a few centuries yet to come. What the Norse shared more greatly outweighed their differences.

Like most societies throughout history, they were driven for a large part by the climate. For example, the Early Middle Ages (6th to 10th centuries) were a period of great strife and conflict, largely in part due to the great cooling after the end of the Roman Empire. That age of cold was deeper than the devastating and more recent Little Ice Age, but shorter in duration. Our Modern Warm Period is merely the result of natural causes returning us from a period of relative cold which happens every thousand years. The Little Ice Age lasted nearly 600 years. The Viking Age's initial period of cold lasted for more like 200 years, with its greatest depth exceeding Little Ice Age cold for less than a century. Yet, it was deep enough and hard enough to spur the Vikings on to greatness.

The High Middle Ages—also known as the Medieval Warm Period—were a period of great prosperity, but the Vikings had already been stirred up. For awhile, they conquered Greenland, growing crops there, where today it is impossible to do so. Ironically, today's news media would have us believe that our modern era is the warmest it has ever been. Clearly, that is not true; history tells us otherwise.

The Vikings established cities and settlements all across Europe. Much as the Greeks had done in an earlier era, the Vikings did not so much create Empire as they, instead, created influence.

Though the Normans of Normandy conquered the land of Northern France, they adopted the language of the locals. Even so, they gave part of their own Scandinavian language to the locals. Later, when the Normans crossed the English Channel, they did the same—adopting the language of the locals, but adding to it their own Norman French, already flavored with its Norse influences.

Like their sagas and heroes, the Norse gods were also a rough and tumble group of individuals with strong character and human frailties.

This book is divided into two main parts. The first will tackle the heroes, their sagas and history. In the second part of the book, we will peer into the heart of Norse religious myth.

Part 1—Heroes and Sagas

*Twelve winters of grief for Hrothgar, king
Of the Danes, sorrow heaped at his door
By hell-forged hands, His misery leaped
The seas, was told and sung in all
Men's ears*

—*Beowulf,* an English epic tale set in Scandinavia

Chapter 1—The Icelandic Sagas

Ingólfr looked back toward his wife and smiled. Soon, their voyage would be over. Soon, they would have a new home free from the threat of the blood feuds they had left behind in Noregi—their ancient homeland amongst the fjords of the North. Little Torstein looked up at him from behind his mother's skirt and admired his fearsome father—a man whose name meant "royal or kingly wolf."

With the fabled island of Garðar Svavarsson in sight, Ingólfr looked down at his high seat pillars—the icons of his status as chieftain—and nodded at the decision he had made the night before.

"Brother," he said to Hjörleifr Hróðmarsson, his step mother's son, "I have prayed to Odin to have his wisdom guide me. I swore an oath to him that if we should sight land, I will lay my pillars upon the sea for the gods to show me where I should build my settlement." He then waved to his brother to help him lift the pillars over the railing and they let them slide into the waters of the cold, north Atlantic.

The year was AD 871. The hardest years of deep cold were behind them. Before them lay the island Naddod had called "snow land," because it had started to sprinkle the white stuff before he had left several decades earlier. Naddod had missed his intended destination, the Faroe Islands, north of the Scots, and had been blown to the northwest. Later, Garðar had been on his way to the Hebrides, off the coast of Scotland, but also had been blown off course. He was the first to circumnavigate the island, confirming that indeed it was an island. That was only a decade earlier than now.

Finally, Ingólfr landed and his thralls and men set up camp. But it was to be a temporary camp. He had to wait for the gods to deliver his pillars to the coast of this island. Only then would he know where to build his new home.

For three years, two of his thralls—Vífill and Karli—searched the coastline, combing every mile time and again, searching for their chieftain's symbols of lordship. Finally, they found the pillars and Ingólfr had his location— a favorable bay on the southwestern coast of the island. There, he gave his settlement the name, Reykjavík, which meant "bay of smokes." The region was surrounded by many, natural, hot springs and the steam rising from them looked like smoke.

Later, Ingólfr found that his step-brother had been killed by his own men. He gave Hjörleifr a proper Norse funeral and then found his step-brother's men had escaped to Vestmannaeyjar (Westman Islands), just south of Iceland. There, the chieftain caught up with the murderers and slew them.

Ingólfr and his family had picked the right century to settle in Iceland. The far more temperate Medieval Warm Period was just starting. Nearly twenty-five percent of the island was covered by forests, so homebuilding would have plenty of resources. In our modern era, only one percent of the island has forests.

Ingólfr's slave, Karli, was not shy about criticizing his chieftain's settlement location. "How ill that we should pass good land, to settle in this remote peninsula."

Settlement continued for another sixty years, at the end of which, all of the arable land had been claimed.

Years later, with the death of his father, Torstein became the new chieftain and eventually founded the first thing—precursor to the Althingi, or national parliament. The Althingi was to become one of the longest running modern parliamentary bodies in the world.

Laws and Blood Feuds

In antiquity, the Norse handled disputes the old-fashioned way—with violence and bloodshed. Insults were numerous and the resulting violence was sometimes more numerous, because one act frequently led to many others in retaliation. One retaliation led to an explosion of counter-retaliations. Peace was sometimes only possible through extinction of one family, or through the realization that extinction was upon them.

To keep things from becoming too chaotic, certain laws were established so that blood feuds could be carried out with some sense of decorum. Perhaps we could call it "ordered chaos."

The Althing (Icelandic Alþingi) was first established AD 930 at Thingvellir (Þingvellir)—"Parliament fields" or "assembly fields." This open assembly was located about forty-five kilometers east of Ingólfr's settlement (now Reykjavík). The assembly was open to all free men. There, they would resolve disputes, hammer out new laws and even grant exceptions to existing laws.

In the days of the Vikings, the family was the key focus of society. If you hurt a free man, you also hurt his family. Blood feuds were common. But sometimes a wrongful death, even if accidental, did not necessarily have to result in violence and retribution. Sometimes the injured party or family could demand *weregild,* or blood money, as restitution. Every person and object of property was given a monetary value. Norwegian *gjeld* and Danish *gæld* meant "debt." The *-gäld* suffix in Swedish had a similar meaning—*gengäld* (exchange or in return), *återgälda* (return favor, retribute), and *vedergälda* (revenge). Of course, if the *weregild* was not paid, a blood feud would almost always ensue.

The madness of this cycle of retaliatory violence should seem obvious. Once started, there is no easy way to stop it, short of forgiveness. But this is not true forgiveness; this is merely a lull in the violence until one side or the other has a more clear advantage and the proper excuse to re-initiate the violence.

From this period of rugged survival and testy conflict, legends of heroes and struggle were born.

The Sagas

The Icelandic Sagas were tales of heroes and their families who settled in Iceland, and of their descendents. Some of the most popular sagas include, Grettis saga, Njáls saga, Egils saga, Laxdæla saga, Gísla saga, and Hrafnkels saga. The stories would include anecdotes of family life, tales of raiding parties to win booty and honor for their family, stories of conquest and even accounts of feuds between families.

In Egil's saga, for instance, the tale spans a century and a half of the family of Kveldulf ("evening wolf"), Egil's grandfather. Harold Fairhair wanted to become king of all Norway and it looked as though he might well accomplish this feat. He called upon Kveldulf to serve in his army, but Kveldulf was now an old man. The king asked for him to send one of his sons, instead, but he refused. Eventually, the strife between Kveldulf's family and that of Harold, would force Kveldulf's family to flee the country and to settle in the newly opened land of Iceland. The bulk of the saga is about Egil, a complex character full of seemingly whimsical violence and great skill at poetry. But when we dig deeper, we find that Egil holds in high regard such values as respect, honor, friendship and loyalty. His violence only comes when these are betrayed.

Egil's saga and several other writings were thought to be the work of Snorri Sturluson (1179–1241), twice voted lawspeaker of the Althingi. He posed the idea that the gods were, in truth, merely mortal men—kings and great heroes of the past who were venerated for generations until each was remembered merely as a divine being, rather than a skillful king.

A note on Icelandic names—most citizens of Iceland used a patronym, rather than a family name, a practice which continues even unto today. This means that the given name is followed by the given name of the person's father. Some surnames in English cultures were originally patronyms, like Peterson (Peter's son). The father's given name has a genitive suffix appended which merely means "son of" (-son) or "daughter of" (-dóttir). This is a holdover from the days of the Vikings when Leif Ericson—the first known European to visit mainland North America—truly was the son of Eric.

The Icelandic sagas were part of the inspiration for Jules Verne's science fiction story, Journey to the Center of the Earth, published 1864. The main character in that story, Professor Lindenbrock of Scotland, found an artifact which included an original saga by Snorri Sturluson. It told of an entrance to the center of our world.

Later, American writer, Edgar Rice Burroughs, was inspired by Verne's work and created his own story named, Pellucidar, first published 1915. The influence of the sagas has run deep in our culture.

In the next chapter, we look at Vikings in the decadent, imperial halls of Byzantium, where the Varangian Guard protected the royal household.

Check out this book!

Preview of Egyptian Mythology Captivating Stories of the Gods, Goddesses, Monsters and Mortals

Introduction: Egypt in Context

Mention the name "Egypt" to most anyone with at least a high school education and it conjures up pictures of the desert, the Nile, palm trees, pyramids and the Sphinx. Today, Egypt is a third-world country rich with petroleum (16% of the nation's economy in 2011), tourism (20%) and industry (20%). The country even makes a substantial income (3%) from their Suez Canal which allows shipping to bypass having to go around Africa for transporting goods between Europe and the Far East.

For the first three thousand years of humanity's shared history, Egypt played a pivotal role in the affairs of man. Its Nile Valley and Delta were one of the cradles of civilization where an organized and settled society was born. The other cradles were found in,

- Mesopotamia—surrounding the Tigris and Euphrates Rivers (modern Iraq),

- Indus Valley—surrounding the Indus River (modern Pakistan),

- China—surrounding the Yellow River,

- Central Andes (modern Peru), and

- Mesoamerica.

Of these six, Egypt and Mesopotamia compete for first place. Both of these regions also vie for first as the birthplace of writing. The Andes and Indus River regions came hundreds of years later. And the earliest known inklings of civilization came more than a thousand years later in China and Mesoamerica.

Humans have been around for at least 200,000 years, so why did civilization start in six different locations so closely spaced in time? It all has to do with climate change.

Egypt and Climate

Egypt has been a nation in one form or another for over five thousand years, all because of the prosperity afforded it by the Nile River and the yearly flooding which made it a center of agriculture. But it wasn't always this way.

We live in an Ice Age which started 2.6 million years ago when both poles had gained ice which persisted throughout the year. Our current interglacial, the Holocene, is one of the dozens of interglacials this Ice Age has seen.

Interglacial periods are relatively short spans of comparative warmth where the polar glaciation recedes. The average interglacial, according to climate scientist W.S. Broecker, is about 11,000 years long. The Holocene is already at least 11,500 years old, so it is older than average. Glacial periods are far longer, averaging 90,000 years in duration. Glacials are brutal on life. Not only is life hard hit by the cold, but cooler oceans make rain scarce, so plants and animals easily die of thirst. Cooler oceans also make carbon dioxide far more scarce in the atmosphere, making it harder for plants to grow.

In the 60s and early 70s, Dr. James Lovelock explored the notion of a lower limit for CO_2 below which plant life would start to die out. In fact, 15,000 BC, CO_2 levels came to within 30 parts-per-million of Lovelock's threshold for mass extinction. Rod Martin, Jr. discusses this in his book, *Red Line—Carbon Dioxide*. Then, about 10,000 BC, massive global warming suddenly made civilization possible. It did this not only by creating more life-affirming warmth, but also by making rain more abundant, and by forcing dissolved carbon dioxide from the oceans back into the atmosphere. All three of these ingredients—warmth, rain and CO_2—made agriculture possible. Without these, growing food on a large scale would have been next to impossible.

Widespread rain was not immediately available, but rain in the highlands of Africa made the Nile River more abundant with water. There have been signs of early agriculture in the Lower Nile Valley as far back as 9,000 BC, but these did not seem to persist. The early part of the Holocene interglacial saw a period of about 3,000 years that was far warmer than our modern warm period—The Holocene Optimum. That greater warmth not only evaporated more water from the oceans, making rain more abundant, a monsoon pattern developed which regularly watered the Sahara, making it green for nearly three millennia. When the Earth cooled, the Sahara once again became a deep, harsh desert. Nomads sought sources of water, many of them settling in the Nile Valley. Not long afterward, the population grew sufficiently to start off what we know of as civilization.

Science and Humility

There is a great deal we do not know about the past, including about Egypt. Not every bit of writing, and not every artifact has been unearthed. And that pertains only to the objects which remain available for us to find. There may be large portions of the past for which evidence no longer exists.

Scientists are required to hold restraint on that great unknown. They call their attitude "skepticism," but this is not quite accurate, according to science philosopher, Rod Martin, Jr. The active ingredients in discovery are restraint, humility and a hunger to know the relative truth of a topic. Scientific method tells us that we should remain unbiased, yet skepticism contains the potent, negative bias of doubt. This works well to counterbalance the natural, positive bias found in fresh college graduates. Many of us fancy ourselves as great problem solvers, but too frequently our first inclinations are wrong simply because we don't yet have sufficient information. Skepticism helps to keep us from jumping to an early conclusion, but it's still a bias.

According to Martin, unfortunately, objective skepticism frequently descends into subjective forms like unsupported dismissiveness and even self-indulgent ridicule. These only get in the way of discovery.

What does this have to do with Egypt? Currently, the study of ancient Egypt "belongs" to a club of self-proclaimed Egyptology experts. If you don't belong to this club, the Egyptian government will frown upon independent investigations. Naturally, this benefits the field by helping to keep it neat and tidy, but new discoveries are quite often anything but orderly. Anyone entertaining wildly new ideas not held by club members is dismissed quite frequently without the need for rigorous support for that dismissal. In other words, even good evidence can become dismissed simply because it doesn't fit the current dogma. This more self-indulgent and subjective form of skepticism quashes discovery and the advancement of science.

This is not merely a problem in Egyptology. All sciences suffer some form of this malady of blind skepticism. North American Anthropology, for instance, endured decades of the "Clovis First" dogma. Scientists were cautioned not to dig below the Clovis horizon (earliest stratum of artifacts found in Clovis, New Mexico). Otherwise, they would be ridiculed and sometimes blocked from receiving funding. Ironically, proof that Clovis was not first would naturally be at lower levels than the Clovis horizon. Such ridicule became an active impediment to scientific progress.

In his bestselling book, *Fingerprints of the Gods,* Graham Hancock notes the work of Robert Schoch in analyzing the Great Sphinx of Giza from a geological perspective. Schoch had noticed that the enclosing wall and core body of the Sphinx had near-vertical erosion patterns consistent with heavy rainfall. But the Sphinx sits at the edge of the Sahara Desert. There has been no consistently heavy rainfall at the Sphinx for at least 6,000 years—ever since the Holocene Optimum. This could mean that the Sphinx and its retaining wall were built thousands of years before the first historical dynasty.

What does this all mean? Any scientist needs to keep an open mind. They need to use restraint not only on accepting new ideas but also on rejecting them, too. Also, it means they need to remain open to rejecting old ideas if new evidence demands such. The key to a proper scientific attitude is to put the evidence first and current dogma a distant third. Second place belongs to brainstorming and creative, critical thinking and imagination.

Mythology's Possible Roots in Fact

Most texts on interpreting ancient Egyptian mythology talk about philosophical metaphors. The figures in myth are taken as metaphors for something found in ordinary life. But Rod Martin, Jr. has suggested that there may be real events and real people behind many of the ancient myths.

Some of the myths, as you will see, sound too incredible to believe. But what if the details of the myths are only symbolically representative of things for which the primitive of 6,000 years ago did not have the adequate vocabulary?

Imagine, for instance, how a primitive hunter-gatherer would describe an empire without having any concept of a nation or tribe. The leader of that empire might become the personification of that nation, and over time, might be described by all of the traits and actions of the empire. Thus, the leader becomes, in the minds of the primitive storyteller, a god or a goddess. Later in the book, we will look through Martin's lens to see what Egyptian mythology might look like as if it were based on real events poorly understood by the chain of storytellers.

What's to Come

The book is broken into three parts:

1. Fantastic Images—Ancient Egyptian myths and legends as we know them today.

2. Factual History—Covering pre-history through classical antiquity.

3. Unraveling Myth—Looking at Egyptian mythology from a fresh perspective.

Check out this book!

Preview of Greek Mythology
A Captivating Guide to the Ancient Gods, Goddesses, Heroes and Monsters

Introduction

Any book on ancient mythology gives us a glimpse into the minds of civilization's pioneers. They were the brave adventurers who explored the unknown territory of possibilities. For them, civilization was yet a mysterious realm with countless directions to go.

Nature is frequently brutal, especially in the cooler climate of an ongoing Ice Age. But the founders of civilization took up the challenge and made the best with what nature had to offer.

We humans got lucky with our current interglacial (warmer phase of an Ice Age) called the Holocene. It started with a rapid warming of +7°C in a period as short as 30 years. This makes our modern, meager warming look weak by comparison. Some interglacial periods have lasted as little as 4,000 years. Ours is already 11,600 years old. All of the Holocene's additional energy gave humans far more life-giving warmth, more essential rain for growing crops and even a boost in carbon dioxide to nudge levels away from the near-extinction levels of the last glacial period.

Understanding the environment of early civilization helps us to appreciate more completely the rugged individualism of those original thinkers. They experienced hardships that most of us could not begin to imagine in the relative comfort of our modern lifestyles.

Even our modern survivalists have it easy compared to those founders of civilization. A survivalist may have tools not available to the humans of 6,000 to 12,000 years ago. At the very least, today's survivalists have knowledge of what is possible that those early primitives could never have dreamed of. They know how things work. Those early humans could only guess. And their guesses were sometimes horribly wrong—even superstitious.

Gods and Monsters

Certainly, a primitive people could come up with a great many wild and strange explanations for the behavior of nature—both the regular cycles and the unique events.

But what if some of the unique events were man made? This is a question that has plagued researcher Rod Martin, Jr. most of his life. Many of the odd and seemingly impossible traits of the ancient gods and monsters become more reasonable when viewed through the lens of a primitive vocabulary. Imagine, for instance, showing a primitive hunter-gatherer a jet aircraft taking off. To them, it might be described as a screaming bird with its wings or tail on fire. An eighteen-wheeler barreling down the highway might become a roaring beast with two bright eyes and a multitude of legs which moved too quickly to be seen clearly.

Historians have long suspected that the mythical centaur may merely have been a human rider on horseback. To the ancient who had never seen a horse and rider, the shock of first contact might have left them unable to grasp such details as two heads and six legs—two legs for the human and four for the horse.

Archaeologists have evidence that peoples who lived north of the Black Sea rode on horseback as early as 6000 to 4000 BC, but we can in no way declare that it is the earliest instance of horse riders. All we can state with any certainty is that this is the earliest known, verifiable instance of horse riders. There is always the possibility that there may have been earlier instances, even if all evidence of such has been destroyed.

Consider for a moment the possibility that an ancient, technological civilization existed long before our own history began. Leggings might become "goat legs" and boots might be seen as "hooves" to the primitive who had never before seen such things. A helmet with horns on top might complete the image of a satyr, or the immortal god Pan.

A patriarchal empire might be understood as a "god," and a matriarchal empire would thus be viewed as a "goddess." Or it might be that factions within an empire might be viewed as individual gods who have the traits of their leaders.

Such a view of myth might not necessarily apply to all of the old stories, but we have to remain prepared for such possibilities when we're searching for answers.

What's Ahead

The broad arc of this book takes us from the dim beginnings of creation as seen in the

Greek mythology. We move through the birth of Titans, their overthrow by the Olympian gods, the gods' dealings with mortals like Paris of Troy, the destruction of Atlantis, Jason and the Golden Fleece, the Trojan War, and into historical times.

This book includes some of the standard views of Greek myth and history, but also tantalizes your imagination with the possibilities that lay behind myth and legend. We won't cover every possible version of every myth, but by the time you're finished with this book, you will have a good appreciation for the nature of Greek mythology and the gods, monsters, and heroes which populate it.

Chapter 1 — Uranus: Betrayal by Cronus

In the very beginning, Chaos (void) ruled the universe. It was the great nothingness. Boring? Of course. Perhaps the sheer blandness of all that empty nothingness forced Gaia (goddess of Earth) to spring into existence from all that emptiness. Close behind, Chaos gave birth to Tartarus (god of the underworld), Eros (god of fertility), Erebus (god of darkness) and Nyx (goddess of night).

Gaia (mother Earth) was so full of fertility that she gave birth to two other primordial gods without having to mate with anyone. Of course, Chaos had no gender, and the universe was relatively empty. Her two sons were named Uranus (god of heaven) and Pontus (god of the ocean).

Feeling lonely, Gaia took her son, Uranus, as her mate. Each night, her son would lay on top of her and mate with her. From these repeated unions, she gave birth to several Titans and monsters. These included Cronus (sometimes spelled Kronos), Oceanus, Tethys, Rhea, Hyperion, Theia, Cruis, Themis, Coeus,

Mnemosyne, Iapetus, Phoebe, the Cyclopes, and the Hecatonchires.

To the Greeks, heaven was selfish. He had a unique relationship with Earth and assumed that he was king of the gods. Was that arrogance? Was it that the other gods didn't care who called themselves "king?" Perhaps so, because nothing is mentioned of any conflict until Uranus started to abuse his children.

Uranus gave selfish love to his mate (his mother and wife). There was passion, but there was also disgust for the children his wife gave him. The youngest of these—the Hecatonchires and Cyclopes—he ended up locking away in his uncle, Tartarus (underworld)—far below the surface of Gaia.

For some reason, Uranus considered these youngest to be particularly hideous. The Hecatonchires, for instance, were three man-like giants, but each with a hundred hands, fifty heads, and massive strength. The Cyclopes were three giants, each with one eye in the centers of their foreheads.

Cousins, Nieces, and Nephews

Over the ages, the universe became more crowded with additional gods and goddesses. The primordials Erebus and Nyx got together and made Aether (God of Light) and Hemera

(Goddess of Day). The Titans had some fun, too. Oceanus took his sister, Tethys, and they together created Amphrite, Dione, Metis, Pleione, Thetis and hundreds of additional, second generation Titans.

Iapetus married one of his nieces—the Oceanid, Clymene—and they together created Atlas, Prometheus, and several others.

Hyperion took his sister, Theia, and they created Helios (sun), Eos (dawn) and Selene (moon).

Coeus married his sister, Phoebe ("shining") and they created Leto who later became the mother of Artemis and Apollo.

Gaia Fed Up with Abuse

Mother Earth became sickened by the abuses of Uranus. She didn't want any more children by that selfish, self-centered tyrant.

From her own body, she plucked a shard of flint and fashioned a great sickle. But the only harvest she had in mind was to reap from Uranus his testicles. This is an ironic concept. Everything else about the earliest gods of the universe—the primordials—is devoid of anything anthropomorphic (man-like). But here, Uranus has the very human physical attribute of male testes.

Perhaps Gaia was a coward for not doing the deed herself, or perhaps she felt that one of her sons would be more capable of finishing the task. She ended up asking all her sons to take up the great sickle. But even her sons were too cowardly to face up to the Great God King Uranus—all except Cronus.

Cronus was the youngest of the first generation Titans. In other words, he was only slightly older than the brothers imprisoned in Tartarus. Perhaps being the youngest who remained free made him struggle harder to keep up with his older siblings. And perhaps, being only slightly older than his imprisoned brothers made him more aware of his own vulnerabilities. Maybe these traits gave him sufficient ambition to overcome any fear.

But Cronus was clever and shrewd. He wasn't one to jump into a task blindly. After all, he did want to survive the attack on his father—heaven itself. So, Cronus hid and ambushed his father, completing the castration and spilling the god's blood onto the Earth (Gaia). From the blood sprang the Giants, the Meliae, and the Furies (Erinyes). Later, the Meliae would give birth to the earliest form of humans.

Tired and disgusted from the task, Cronus tossed his father's genitals into the ocean (Pontus). Such potent energy remained in the godly organ that the sea whipped up an extreme froth (sea foam, aphros) and from it was born Aphrodite Ourania (goddess of spiritual love).

Uranus groaned in agony at the betrayal and condemned all of those of his children who were currently visible—the ones not in Tartarus—calling his sons, "Titanes Theoi," which means "straining gods." From this curse, we get the word "Titan."

With Uranus made impotent, the Hecatonchires and Cyclopes were freed from Tartarus. Gaia was relieved that her youngest sons were finally liberated.

Cronus, feeling the ambitious pride swell within him, took advantage of the situation and claimed the universe as his own. He now became the new king of the gods.

But Cronus had not performed the task requested by his mother and grandmother, Gaia, in order to free his younger brothers. Quite the contrary, Cronus despised the Cyclopes and Hecatonchires as much as his father and brother, Uranus, did. At the first opportunity, Cronus put his six younger brothers back in Tartarus, greatly angering his mother at the betrayal.

Despite his arrogance and cruelty, in some respects, Cronus's rule was viewed as a

Golden Age. During his time as king of the gods, the Meliae gave birth to the first humans. These men lived for thousands of years but maintained a youthful appearance. This was a time of tranquility and nobility of spirit, and the young, fragile race of humans mingled with the gods.

With his scythe, Cronus became associated with the harvest and its celebration. His rule was filled with abundance.

Check out this book!

Free Bonus from Captivating History (Available for a Limited time)

Hi History Lovers!

Now you have a chance to join our exclusive history list so you can get your first history ebook for free as well as discounts and a potential to get more history books for free! Simply visit the link below to join.

Captivatinghistory.com/ebook

Also, make sure to follow us on:

Twitter: @Captivhistory

Facebook: Captivating History: @captivatinghistory

Make sure to check out more books by

Make sure to check out more books from Matt Clayton and Captivating History

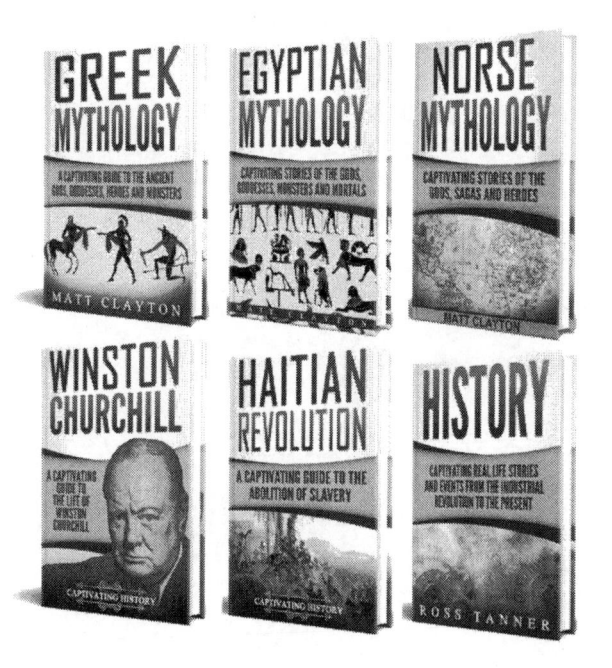

Made in the USA
Middletown, DE
10 January 2018